Goalkeeping Drills

volume one

Drills for improving agility, reaction speed and conditioning.

by
Gerd Thissen
Klaus Röllgen

Library of Congress Cataloging - in - Publication Data

by Röllgen, Klaus and Thissen, Gerd
Goalkeeping Drills: volume one
Drills for improving agility, reaction speed and conditioning.
ISBN No. 1-890946-40-0
Library of Congress Catalog Number 00-101831
Copyright © April 2000

Originally printed in Germany - 1999 by Carolus-Sportverlag

Art Direction/Book Layout
Kimberly N. Bender

Diagrams
Karlheinz Grindler

Photos
Presse-Foto-Dienst

Original Layout in Germany
Carlus-Sportverlag

Editing and Proofing
Bryan R. Beaver

Printed by
DATA REPRODUCTIONS

REEDSWAIN INC
612 Pughtown Road • Spring City • Pennsylvania 19475
1-800-331-5191• www.reedswain.com

Goalkeeping Drills
volume one

Drills for improving agility, reaction speed and conditioning.

by
Gerd Thissen
Klaus Röllgen

published by
REEDSWAIN INC

Foreword

I have often wished that I had a book of coaching drills for goalkeepers. When I watch training sessions, I am always surprised to see how little specific work is carried out with goalkeepers. Often the only time that a goalkeeper is called on to show what he can do is when a drill finishes up with a shot at goal. This cannot be described as systematic goalkeeper coaching.

Even coaches who devote time to their goalkeepers are amazingly lacking in ideas. Perhaps the soccer theorists have left coaches in the dark.

I am therefore grateful to Gerd Thissen and Klaus Röllgen for this contribution to meeting a clear need. This easily accessible book will stimulate many a voluntary helper to accept the role of goalkeeper coach. This aspect of the book is of particular significance for those at the lower or junior levels of the game, who may have to supervise the training of 15 players alone.

I hope that this book will become widely accepted by coaches at all levels and will lead to an improvement in the quality of goalkeeper coaching.

Egidius Braun
President of the German Soccer Association

We do not want to exaggerate. The soccer world is all too familiar with extravagant claims. However, it can be said with every justification that a goalkeeper occupies an important and special position in a soccer team. This should be reflected in goalkeeper coaching. It should be varied, focused and tough.

This book contains all the elements of good goalkeeper conditioning. I congratulate the authors and hope that coaches and goalkeepers will take its lessons to heart in daily practice.

Dettmar Cramer
German professional league, German Soccer Association and FIFA coach.

General and goalkeeper-specific general exercises - a basic and essential part of modern goalkeeper conditioning. A goalkeeper's defensive actions require a high level of flexibility, agility, dexterity and coordination, as for example when he is at full stretch to block a low shot with his foot.

Table of Contents

Foreword   i

Introduction   1

Key aspects of the drills   2

Goalkeeper conditioning   3

Explanation of the drill descriptions   11

Key to diagrams   16

Drills

Handling the ball   17

Warming-up   29

Abdominal muscles   38

Back muscles   43

Arm muscles   45

Leg muscles   46

Speed off the mark   47

Catching technique   49

Agility   53

Endurance   94

Take-off strength   115

Reaction speed   130

Introduction

Soccer goalkeeping requires good technique, a good tactical understanding and good physical fitness. Conditioning must repeatedly focus on all of these aspects, both individually and in combination, to enable goalkeepers to develop to their full potential. Unfortunately this is not always the case. Many coaches and instructors tend to concentrate on just a few elements of goalkeeping, which almost invariably concern only goal-line skills. Important aspects such as dominating the penalty area are rarely dealt with.

This book describes a number of widely varied drills, which are intended to improve the individual **key aspects of goalkeeping**. It contains a large selection of drills as well as describing various aids (tires, for example) with which imaginative goalkeeper training sessions can be devised.

The following drills are not meant to form an integrated coaching program. The intention is to give coaches a wide and varied selection of drills, so that they can plan their own programs to achieve their own objectives. The drills have been devised primarily with amateur soccer players in mind. Most of them involve only one goalkeeper, although a few are for two goalkeepers. A number of drills simulate match conditions and require the participation of outfield players. Drills that simply require the participation of a goalkeeper as an aid to improving the shooting skills of outfield players are not included.

It is assumed that the goalkeepers who perform the drills have already acquired the various elements of goalkeeping technique and have mastered the main principles of goalkeeping tactics. In principle the drills are within the capabilities of the average amateur goalkeeper.

The layout of the book derives from the wish to give the reader a visual impression of the described drill, thus making it easier to understand. Each description is accompanied by a number of diagrams, showing the key phases of the drill. This should enable coaches and instructors to translate them more easily into everyday coaching practice.

Key aspects of the drills

The **key aspects** of the following drills are derived from the **conditional, technical** and **tactical factors** that characterize **modern goalkeeping**. Even when outfield players are involved, only the goalkeeping aspects of the drill are described. Some of the drills are organized and simplified in such a way as to make them easier to understand.
The following **key aspects** are referred to in the practical part of the book.

Technique	Tactics	Conditioning
• Handling the ball	• Positional play	• Speed off the mark
• Catching technique	• Dominating the penalty area	• Reaction speed
• Gathering low balls	• Winning the ball	• Endurance
• Diving forward to catch the ball	• Moving off the line at the right moment	• Take-off strength
• Rolling sideways	• One against one situations	• Agility
• Diving to stop low shots	• Using technical and tactical skills in simulated match situations	• Coordination
• Diving to stop medium-high shots		
• Diving to stop high to medium-high shots		
• Punching (one hand and two hands)		
• Deflecting the ball		
• Throwing and kicking the ball into play		
• Kicking with the instep		
• Sidefooting the ball		
• Defending with the feet		

The general warming-up drills can only fulfill their purpose if they are carried out for the correct length of time. Otherwise the emphasis is on the following key aspects.

Endurance is only mentioned and singled out as a special conditioning objective in connection with a few drills, as endurance can be made the main aspect of almost any drill by increasing its duration.

When the focus is on take-off strength, the words "running take-off from one foot" will be added in parentheses when this is the main aspect of the drill.

The muscular conditioning aspects mentioned in connection with many drills are of secondary importance and are usually attributable to changes of position and posture during the course of the drill. The exclusive gymnastic objective is strengthening the muscles.

Special conditioning

A key characteristic of goalkeeper conditioning is that it is mainly carried out **individually**. It can thus be regarded as special conditioning. In contrast to outfield players, goalkeepers carry out drills almost exclusively concerned with acquiring and developing the special skills and abilities they need to play in their position in the team. Like every other member of the team, the goalkeeper must acheive a certain basic level in the areas of **conditioning, technique** and **tactics** to be successful. Moreover he must have **special qualities** to be able to perform the tasks and meet the demands associated with his position. It is therefore necessary for a goalkeeper to be coached **separately** and **individually**. Comprehensive, varied and targeted coaching must be used to build up and develop the goalkeeper's innate movement skills. Only then can a goalkeeper acquire the **understanding of his role** that will enable him to carry out the basic tasks associated with his position within the framework of the team as a whole and the system it plays. Through appropriate **conditioning experience** he learns the basic principles associated with his position and is able to appreciate his conditional, technical and tactical resources correctly, so that he can apply them in simulated match situations and in real matches.

Organizational framework

For most coaches, goalkeeper coaching poses **problems of both content and organization**. During a training session a coach must keep both outfield players and goalkeepers busy with a variety of tasks. Because he cannot supervise both groups at the same time, he must ensure that there is no slacking on the part of the group with which he is not directly involved at any given time. Usually the goalkeepers find themselves left to their own devices for part of the time or simply have to stand around with nothing to do. The time that can be devoted to issues that are of direct relevance to goalkeepers, or to eliminating individual weaknesses, is short. Good organization is the best way to remedy this shortcoming. The following **organizational options** are available for goalkeeper training sessions.

- The coach spends time with the goalkeepers before or after the main training session.

In this case the coach might devote 45 minutes to working with his goal-keepers without having to observe his outfield players at the same time. The weather plays a role here. To avoid any risk of the goalkeepers catching a cold, they should be closely involved in the main training session when the weather is poor (when it is raining, during the winter, etc.). Periods of rest when wearing clothing that is soaked with rain or sweat should be avoided. If a session for goalkeepers is held after the main training session, the goalkeepers can be allowed to turn up in time for the second part of the main session. They can then warm up on their own before joining in with the other players.

- Goalkeeper conditioning is integrated into the main training session

The goalkeepers participate in the warming-up and the general conditioning work of the outfield players. Goalkeeper-specific aspects are introduced during shooting practice, when the goalkeepers are confronted with situations similar to those in a real match.

- The goalkeepers work on their own in line with a conditioning plan drawn up by the coach while the coach works with the other players.

This independent manner of working requires self-discipline and responsibility from the goalkeepers. The plan must be carefully prepared by the coach. The coach must discuss the drills with the goalkeepers to ensure that they are thoroughly familiar with them. To prevent any misunderstandings, the goalkeepers should have already carried out the drills under the supervision of the coach. To achieve his conditioning objectives the coach must specify the duration of the periods of work and rest.

It is worth remarking that excessive rivalry or feelings of antagonism between the first and second goalkeepers can impede this independent approach or even make it impossible. In this case it is advisable to give each goalkeeper his own conditioning plan and allow him to work independently.

- The coach supervises a complete training session with the goalkeepers.

The training session can be held on the same day as the outfield players' session (for example 2 hours beforehand), or on another day.

- While the chief coach supervises the main training session, the assistant coach supervises the goalkeepers.

If the training ground is big enough, this is the best way of ensuring intensive and effective goalkeeper conditioning. Moreover the goalkeepers can immediately be called upon to participate in the main training session when necessary.

There is no general answer to the question of which of these options is the best. In practice all of these options can be used. Naturally, circumstances at professional clubs differ from those in the amateur game. Amateur coaches are dependent on the free time that they and their goalkeepers can make available for additional training sessions. Ideally a goalkeeper requires the intensive supervision and help of a coach or assistant coach. Obviously this is not always feasible. It is, however, of considerable importance that a coach makes the best use of the available time and resources to plan a conditioning regime that will motivate his goalkeepers as much as possible. **Skillful alternation between the above forms of organization** can contribute to this.

General principles

- The intensity of the drills, the length of the recuperation periods, the number of repeats, etc. should always be harmonized to the level of conditioning of the goalkeeper and the coaching objectives.

In principle, the objectives of many drills can only be achieved if the drills are carried out intensively. Many of the drill descriptions indicate the suggested number of repeats in the form of the **number of balls** (for example, **6 balls = 6 repeats**). For drills carried out by pairs of players, the suggested **number of repeats** may be indicated directly (for example, **swap tasks after 5 repeats**).

- Adjust the degree of difficulty of the drill to the goalkeeper's level of conditioning and ability.

- Gradually increase the degree of difficulty and complexity of the drills, while gradually introducing drills that make higher technical and tactical demands on the goalkeeper.

- Training for technique and reaction speed should only be carried out when the goalkeepers are warmed up and rested.

Coordination conditioning

Goalkeeper-specific coordination conditioning involves **drills with the ball** that focus on a specific aspect of technique, supplemented by **additional tasks**. These additional tasks precede a defensive action by the goalkeeper. These may include various **forms of running** (forward, backward, sideways, hopping, etc.), different paths (straight line, zigzag, slalom, curve, etc.) and a variety of **positional and postural changes** (turning, rolling, jumping, goalkeeper lying face down, on his back, front, side, etc.) either individually or in combination. Variety is of the essence, so that the goalkeeper is faced with constantly changing challenges to his sense of orientation or balance, his reaction speed, etc. This book contains numerous examples and variations.

Competitive drills

Competitive drills can be used to make goalkeeper conditioning more varied and interesting. In addition, the **competitive element** of the drill stimulates the goalkeeper's motivation and readiness to learn and perform well. A genuinely competitive situation is created, which promotes the goalkeeper's will to win and creates opportunities to use the techniques and tactics he has learned and practiced. The main objective of these competitive drills is to give the goalkeeper the opportunity to employ his abilities to the limit, especially in one-against-one situations. This means that the goalkeeper must always have a reasonable chance of saving the ball when the coach or outfield player tries to score. Despite the competitive element, the emphasis is on the **goalkeeper's performance** and not the shooting ability of the outfield player or the coach.

General exercises for goalkeepers

Keeping goal makes considerable demands on a goalkeeper's athletic prowess. Strength, speed and endurance have to be allied with robustness, agility, dexterity and excellent coordination to enable a goalkeeper to respond adequately to the challenges of all types of match situations by diving, rolling, jumping, getting back quickly onto his feet and reacting instantaneously without risking injury, irrespective of the weather and pitch conditions. **General and goalkeeper-specific exercises** are therefore a basic and indispensable part of modern goalkeeper conditioning. Gymnastic exercises for the arm, leg and trunk muscles and the associated ligaments, tendons and joints, as well as whole-body exercises, build up the goalkeeper's body in general and can be targeted on facilitating the many movements that a goalkeeper may need to make. One example is the leg stretch to block a low ball. Gymnastic exercises suitable for working out alone or in pairs, with or without aids, can be incorporated into the warming-up phase or recuperation periods as a supplementary active element of goalkeeper training sessions. A few gymnastic exercises are described in this book. They are carried out with the help of a ball and should make the training sessions more positive and enjoyable for the players. The conditioning effect is usually based on short, intensive periods of work involving a lot of movement. This effect can be enhanced by using a medicine ball instead of an ordinary soccer ball.

Outfield play

Since the recent introduction of the backpass rule, greater demands have been made on the ability of the goalkeeper to function as an outfield player. As well as practicing their own specific skills, goalkeepers should train together with the other players as often as possible to learn **ball technique** and the **tactical aspects of outfield play**. When a goalkeeper plays in an outfield position during a training session he learns about aspects of play such as the different lines of the ball and the outfield players' runs and patterns of movement. This can help him to anticipate an attacker's intentions. The experience that a goalkeeper gains in this way gives him a better understanding of the demands of specific outfield positions and helps him to improve his cooperation with his teammates and adjust more readily to the opposing team's attacking tactics.

Indoor training sessions

During autumn and winter the weather and the condition of the pitch may considerably restrict the opportunities for goalkeepers to train outdoors. If the pitch is frozen, for example, there is a much higher risk of sustaining an injury when diving to stop the ball. Indoor training for goalkeepers is often regarded unfavorably and is viewed as a last resort. Nevertheless, a gymnasium presents opportunities that are either not present outdoors or could only be made available with considerable effort. With appropriate **organizational preparation**, indoor sessions can supplement and enhance outdoor training sessions. The focus should be on the following **key conditioning aspects**.

Gymnastic exercises

A varied and comprehensive range of gymnastic drills and exercises, both with and without apparatus, is available for goalkeepers. Gymnastic balls, medicine balls, bars and clubs can be used as well as mats, wall bars, etc. Working with gymnastic apparatus increases the goalkeeper's motivation as well as the effect of the individual exercises. The overall result is that all aspects of the goalkeeper's physique are improved. He can carry out exercises while lying face down or on his back without any fear of catching a cold. A richly varied conditioning program can be put together by combining different elements in different ways, with the focus on developing his agility, dexterity and mobility.

General and specific physical conditioning

A gymnasium offers almost unlimited opportunities for improving a goalkeeper's physical condition. All kinds of walking, running, hopping, climbing and crawling exercises can be carried out. Running and jumping, working with a medicine ball, different types of circuit training, etc. permit varied and targeted physical conditioning.

Technique

Despite the hard floor, almost all goal-stopping techniques can be practiced in the gymnasium in a variety of ways. The use of mats on the floor, in combination with padding in the goalkeeper's shorts and sweater, make falling and diving possible to almost the same extent as on a grass pitch. A ball can also be suspended from the supports used for gymnastic rings to allow the goalkeepers to practice one and two-fisted punching.

Speed of reaction and movement

Large areas of the walls of the gymnasium can often be used for shooting practice. They offer many possibilities for goalkeepers to sharpen their reaction speed and to practice alone. They can also be used to develop and improve catching skills.

Coordination

The markings and apparatus in the gymnasium offer numerous organizational possibilities for practicing coordination skills. For example, a goal-keeper can be required to complete a small obstacle course before preventing another player from scoring.

Simple and available aids and apparatus

The use of different aids and apparatus for goalkeeper training sessions simplifies the coach's task of making the sessions varied and interesting. The structure of the sessions can be modified in many ways and can be targeted on developing particular skills and abilities. The aids and apparatus also give goalkeepers **more options for working on their own**, especially for **practicing technique**. In general, the use of complex structural aids should be avoided. Everything that can be found in **any sports facility** should be used, e.g. a suspended ball, a sandpit, the pitch, the steps of the bleachers, a "shooting wall." Other aids that can be easily obtained include weighted vests, dumbbells, expanders, hurdles, swingballs, rugby balls or used tires.

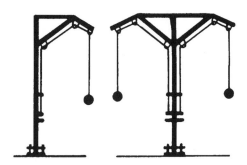

A suspended ball is an excellent aid for goalkeepers practicing alone. It is especially suitable for learning how to punch the ball with one or both fists. Because this can be practiced repeatedly, it is an especially effective method of learning and improving this skill. A suspended ball can also be used to condition a goalkeeper's take-off strength. The cord to which the ball is attached should be as long as possible to ensure that the goalkeeper acquires a good punching technique. The long swing of the ball allows the goalkeeper to concentrate on his punching technique and to become used to assessing the path of the ball.

The pitch, the bleachers, weighted vests and hurdles can be used in a variety of ways during goalkeeper training sessions. **Diving** should first be practiced in a sandpit to break down any inhibitions the goalkeeper may have and avoid accidents. A sandpit also provides an excellent soft surface for **conditioning and take-off exercises**. For this reason, many of the drills that are carried out on grass should also be carried out in a sandpit.

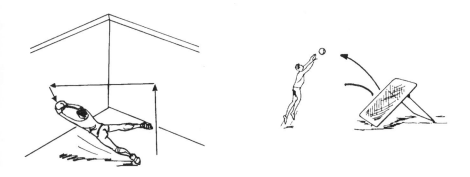

Part of the wall of the changing room or the wall around the sports ground can be used as a shooting wall. If there is no grass in front of the wall, sand can be spread to reduce the risk of injury. If a portable shooting wall made of wood or some other equipment is used, it should not cushion the ball on impact and thus rob it of some of its momentum. A goalkeeper can **practice alone** in a variety of ways with such a wall. In particular he can develop and improve his **reaction speed** and **catching technique**. A shooting wall with an uneven surface increases the degree of difficulty for the goalkeeper. The direction of the rebound cannot be predicted and the goalkeeper has to react with the speed of lightning.

A new variation of the shooting wall is the **kickback**. The angle of the rebound surface can be varied, so the angle of rebound also varies. This provides the coach with numerous options to suit the level of ability of the goalkeeper.

An oval **rugby ball** can be used to improve the goalkeeper's **catching technique** and **reaction speed**. The ball is also relatively heavy, so the goalkeeper has to grasp it firmly when he catches it. The shape of the ball makes its flight more irregular and difficult to gauge than that of a round ball.

Used **tires** are very worthwhile aids for goalkeeper training sessions. They can be stacked to form an obstacle that the goalkeeper has to dive over, and they are used above all to improve the goalkeeper's **endurance, take-off strength, agility** and **dexterity**. Since there is little danger of suffering an injury when diving over tires, goalkeepers easily overcome any psychological inhibitions they may have about diving over other forms of obstacle (e.g. hurdles).

Explanation of the drill descriptions

The descriptions of the **basic drills** are organized in accordance with a **basic structure**. The descriptions are subdivided into the following elements: **Key aspects, Starting Position, Phase 1, Phase 2**, etc., **Number of participants** and **Equipment**. In some cases **variations** of the basic drill are included. Each variation is described individually. The starting position, phase 1, phase 2, etc. and variations are illustrated by the use of **diagrams**.

Example

Key aspects	
• Catching technique	• Take-off strength
• Agility	• Reaction speed
• Diving to stop low shots	• Catching the ball securely
• Diving to stop high to medium-high shots	**Variation 2**
• Rolling away to the side	• Two-fisted punching

3-4 yds.

Starting position
The goalkeeper stands 3 or 4 yards from the coach, who is holding the ball.

Phase 1
The coach drops the ball and kicks it hard to the goalkeeper, varying the height and direction of the ball.

Phase 2
The goalkeeper must catch or stop the shots, which can come at him at all heights and be directed at his body or to his right or left. He must use the correct catching technique and secure the ball properly after catching it. He throws the ball back into the coach's hands and then resumes his starting position, so that the coach can immediately kick the ball to him again.

Variations
1. The goalkeeper kneels instead of standing, so the coach has to take care not to kick the ball too high or too wide of him.
2. The coach kicks the ball straight at the goalkeeper and the goalkeeper punches it away with both fists.

• Catching technique

Participants:	1 goalkeeper	Equipment:	1 ball
	Coach	Variation 2:	5 balls

The text in the **margin** is intended as an aid to the reader when he is searching for the correct type of drill.

Example: • **Catching technique**

This text indicates how the drills are organized. It shows the **specific objective of the described drill**. This may be:

- Handling the ball
- Catching technique
- Agility
- Endurance
- Take-off strength
- Reaction speed
- Defending with the feet
- Punching the ball

- Deflecting the ball
- Winning the ball
- Throwing and kicking the ball into play
- Positional play
- One against one situations
- Dominating the penalty area

Each of these objectives can in turn be assigned to one of the following categories:

- General exercises with the ball
- Competitive situations and simulated match situations
- Competitive games
- Conditioning aids

Detailed information on the technical, tactical and conditioning objectives of the drill is given under the heading **Key aspects**. These key aspects refer to the basic drill.

Example

Key aspects	
• Catching technique	• Rolling away to the side
• Agility	• Take-off strength
• Diving to stop low shots	• Reaction speed
• Diving to stop high to medium-high shots	• Catching the ball securely

The sequence of key aspects indicates to some extent the weighting of the objectives. The most important aspect is positioned first. If the basic drill is supplemented by one or more variations, their key aspects are also listed. The key aspects already listed for the basic drill are not repeated, as they usually also to apply for the variations.

Example

Key aspects
- Catching technique
- Agility
- Diving to stop low shots
- Diving to stop high to medium-high shots

- Rolling away to the side
- Take-off strength
- Reaction speed
- Catching the ball securely

Variation
- Two-fisted punching

The information needed to understand the selected drill is given under the headings **Starting position, Phase 1, Phase 2**, etc. and, for the variations, under **Variation** or **Variations**. The texts under these headings, together with the **illustrations**, form a complete unit. The text of each drill is formulated as an accompaniment to the diagrams and can be used as an aid to a **verbal explanation** of the drill. This is important for coaches and instructors, who must not only be able to understand a drill before putting it into practice but must also be able to explain it precisely to their players and point out any difficulties they may encounter. The ability to describe a drill to the goalkeeper and to translate the description into practice is essential if the objective of the drill is to be achieved. This is why the illustrations are accompanied by detailed and comprehensive descriptions. Each drill should be regarded as complete in itself. The text contains no references to other drills. This makes a certain amount of repetition unavoidable. Each description refers to possible difficulties that may be encountered and to opportunities for emphasizing specific aspects. As already mentioned, these are important for the proper implementation of the drill and for the targeted realization and intensification of the effects of the drill. The **variations** usually involve a higher level of complexity or difficulty. They demand more from the goalkeeper. If more than one variation is given, they are listed in order of increasing difficulty.

The descriptions also include information on the number of **participants** and the **equipment** needed, including goal area, half of the pitch, goal, barrier, etc.

Example

Participants:	1 goalkeeper	Equipment:	1 ball
	Coach	Variation 2:	5 balls

The **basic structure** of a drill can be varied as required. Markings can be changed or added. Flags, cones or balls can be used as goalposts. The locations where the drills are carried out can be varied. The specified number of balls, size of goal, distance between coach and goalkeeper and between goalkeeper and ball should always be understood as guidelines. Coaches are free to make changes in line with their own ideas. In many cases a second goalkeeper can take over the role of the coach, and in his turn the coach can assume the role of the second goalkeeper if necessary. The basic structure can thus be followed closely or broadened at will to include or focus on individual objectives related to the goalkeeper's strengths and weaknesses. With a little initiative and imagination the basic drills can be used as a model for new drills or variations. Many variations have not been included in the book, since its purpose is to introduce as many different types of drills as possible rather than elaborate at length on just a few.

Key to diagrams

Path of the ball

Path of the player running with the ball

Path of player running off the ball

o   Ball

Marker flag

Line marking part of the pitch (goal line, side line, center line, lines marking the goal area or penalty area)

Direction of turn

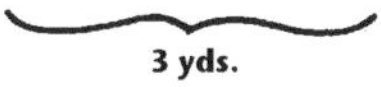

Distance

3 yds.

Defender

Outfield player, attacker

Neutral midfield player

Key aspects
- Handling the ball
- Agility and dexterity
- Coordination
- Handling the ball with the stronger and the weaker hand

The goalkeeper bounces the ball very high, very low, or to a medium height with his right or left hand, with both hands or with his right and left hand alternately. While doing so he can stand, squat, sit, kneel or lie face down.

The goalkeeper bounces the ball very high, very low, or to a medium height in a circle around his body with his right and left hand while standing, squatting, sitting or kneeling.

The goalkeeper bounces the ball back and forth through his legs while standing on the spot.

The goalkeeper jumps in the air and bounces the ball backward through his legs with both hands. While jumping he turns through 180 degrees so that when he lands he can catch the ball as it bounces back up.

Handling the ball

| Participant: 1 goalkeeper | Equipment: 1 ball |

Key aspects
- Handling the ball
- Agility and dexterity
- Coordination
- Handling the ball with the stronger and the weaker hand

The goalkeeper bounces the ball on the ground with both hands, quickly makes a complete clockwise or counterclockwise turn and catches the ball at hip height.

The goalkeeper throws the ball up into the air in front of his body, quickly makes a complete clockwise or counterclockwise turn and catches the ball.

The goalkeeper bounces the ball from his right hand to his left and back again while standing or moving slowly forward. As he does so he swings one leg upward so that the ball bounces under it.

The goalkeeper swings one leg upward while standing on the spot or moving slowly forward and switches the ball from one hand to the other under his thigh.

• Handling the ball

Participant: 1 goalkeeper   **Equipment:** 1 ball

Key aspects
- Handling the ball
- Agility and dexterity
- Coordination
- Handling the ball with the stronger and the weaker hand

The goalkeeper bounces the ball from his left hand to the right and vice versa. As he catches the ball he turns his hand so that the ball remains on his palm. As he bounces the ball he turns his palm to face the ground again.

The goalkeeper lies in the press-up position, supporting himself on one hand, and bounces the ball with the other hand.

The goalkeeper lies in the press-up position, supporting himself on one hand and bounces the ball with his free hand. After each bounce he switches hands.

The goalkeeper lies with his body raised off the ground, supporting himself on one hand, and throws the ball into the air with his free hand. Each time the ball is in the air he switches hands to support himself on the throwing hand and catch the ball with the other.

The goalkeeper lies on his back, holding the ball with both hands above his chest. He pushes the ball up into the air, springs to his feet and catches the ball before it falls to the ground.

● Handling the ball

| **Participant:** 1 goalkeeper | **Equipment:** 1 ball |

Key aspects
- Handling the ball
- Agility and dexterity
- Coordination
- Handling the ball with the stronger and the weaker hand

The goalkeeper passes the ball from hand to hand in a circle around his body at hip height.

The goalkeeper raises his arms straight above his head and passes the ball back and forth from hand to hand with his fingers spread wide.

The goalkeeper holds his upper arms pressed against his sides with his lower arms held parallel to the ground and passes the ball back and forth from hand to hand with his fingers spread wide.

The goalkeeper lies on his back and passes the ball from hand to hand in a circle around his body.

The goalkeeper throws the ball over his shoulder from behind his back with one hand and catches it in front of his chest with the other.

• Handling the ball

Participant: 1 goalkeeper   **Equipment:** 1 ball

20

Key aspects
- Handling the ball
- Agility and dexterity
- Coordination
- Handling the ball with the stronger and the weaker hand

The goalkeeper stands with his legs spread wide apart and his body bent forward. He holds the ball between his legs with both hands, one pressing against it from the front and one from the back. The goalkeeper releases the ball, quickly switches hands, and catches the ball before it touches the ground.

The goalkeeper stands with his legs spread wide apart and his body bent forward. He holds the ball behind his legs at knee height with both hands. He throws the ball forward through his legs and catches it with both hands at knee height in front of his legs.

The goalkeeper stands with his legs spread wide apart and his body bent forward. Holding the ball with both hands, he extends his arms through his legs from front to back, then throws the ball upward and forward and quickly stands upright to catch the ball above his head.

The goalkeeper stands with his legs spread apart and passes the ball back and forth from hand to hand in a wide arc above his head, bending as far to the right and left as he can.

Handling the ball

Participant: 1 goalkeeper	Equipment: 1 ball

21

The goalkeeper uses his right or left fist, both fists or each fist alternately to balance the ball in the air above his head while standing, sitting, moving forward or moving backward.

The goalkeeper holds the ball in both hands with his fingers spread wide and bounces it repeatedly against the goalpost above head height. Alternatively he can use one or both fists to perform the same task.

The goalkeeper uses both hands to throw the ball against the crossbar as he moves sideways in a series of small jumps across the face of the goal.

The goalkeeper stands with his legs slightly apart, bends his trunk backward and pushes his hips forward. He lifts the ball over his head from front to back and lets go of it behind his back. He turns quickly through 180 degrees and catches the ball before it touches the ground.

• Handling the ball

Participant: 1 goalkeeper   **Equipment:** 1 ball

The standing goalkeeper bounces the ball on the ground with his right or left hand or with each hand alternately. Without ceasing to bounce the ball he sinks into a crouching, sitting or kneeling position or lies face down.

The goalkeeper sits on the ground with his legs spread apart and bounces the ball on the ground between his legs with both hands. After several bounces he bounces the ball hard against the ground so that it springs to the front or side. He then leaps up and catches it before it touches the ground again.

The goalkeeper keeps the ball bouncing with one hand while walking, running or skipping.

While standing on the spot or running forward, the goalkeeper throws the ball up and over his head from left to right or right to left, then catches it as high in its flight as he can and clasps it safely to his chest.

• Handling the ball

| Participant: 1 goalkeeper | Equipment: 1 ball |

Key aspects
- Handling the ball
- Agility and dexterity
- Coordination
- Handling the ball with the stronger and the weaker hand

With his fingers spread wide, the goalkeeper uses his right or left hand, both hands or each hand alternately to balance the ball in the air above his head while standing, sitting, moving forward or moving backward.

The goalkeeper tries to keep the ball in the air using his upper and lower arms and his shoulders.

The goalkeeper bounces the ball on the ground using his right or left fist, both fists or each fist alternately, while standing on the spot or moving forward or backward.

• **Handling the ball**

Participant: 1 goalkeeper   **Equipment:** 1 ball

Key aspects
- Handling the ball
- Agility and dexterity
- Coordination
- Handling the ball with the stronger and the weaker hand

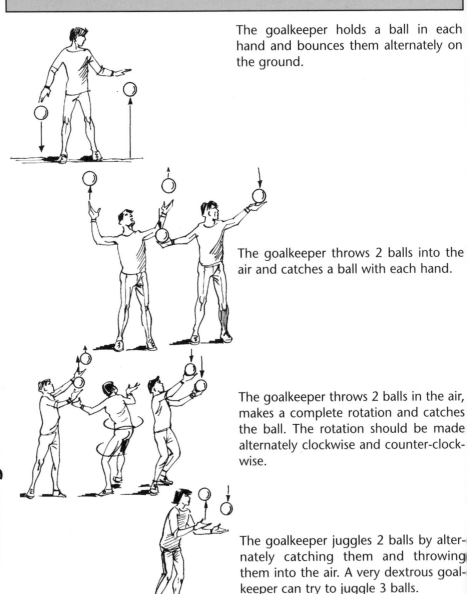

The goalkeeper holds a ball in each hand and bounces them alternately on the ground.

The goalkeeper throws 2 balls into the air and catches a ball with each hand.

The goalkeeper throws 2 balls in the air, makes a complete rotation and catches the ball. The rotation should be made alternately clockwise and counter-clockwise.

The goalkeeper juggles 2 balls by alternately catching them and throwing them into the air. A very dextrous goalkeeper can try to juggle 3 balls.

Handling the ball

Participant: 1 goalkeeper   **Equipment:** 2-3 balls

25

The coach and the goalkeeper stand facing each other 1 to 2 yards apart. They hold their arms extended toward each other, each with a ball in the right (or left) hand and throw the balls to each other simultaneously.

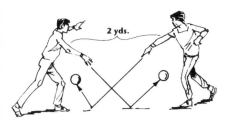

The coach and the goalkeeper stand facing each other 2 yards apart. Each has a ball. They bounce the balls to each other simultaneously and catch them.

The coach and the goalkeeper stand facing each other 2 yards apart. Each holds a ball in each hand. They throw both balls to each other simultaneously.

• Handling the ball

Participants:	1 goalkeeper	Equipment:	2-4 balls
	Coach		

26

The goalkeeper clasps one ball to his chest with one hand. The coach throws another ball to him, which he catches with his free hand. The coach throws the ball from a distance of 2 yards in various trajectories (flat; high to the left or right or above the goalkeeper's head; at the goalkeeper's body, etc.).

The goalkeeper holds his arms out to the side, parallel to the ground. He holds a ball in each hand. The coach stands 3 yards in front of him and throws a ball to one of the goalkeeper's hands. The goalkeeper throws the ball in the receiving hand to the coach and catches the ball thrown by the coach.

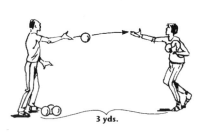

The coach stands 3 yards in front of the goalkeeper and throws 4 to 6 balls in sequence to him. The goalkeeper has to catch all of them without putting any of them down or allowing any of them to fall. Nor may he hold any of the balls clamped between his legs.

• Handling the ball

Participants:	1 goalkeeper	Equipment:	2-6 balls
	Coach		

Key aspects
• Handling the ball
• Agility and dexterity
• Coordination
• Handling the ball with the stronger and the weaker hand

The 2 goalkeepers stand 4 yards apart. They throw the ball to each other with the right and left hand alternately. Only one hand can be used to catch the ball. The ball is thrown back with the hand that caught it.

The 2 goalkeepers stand 2 yards apart. They punch the ball to each other, using either one or both fists, and try to keep the ball in the air for as long as possible.

The 2 goalkeepers stand 4 yards apart. Goalkeeper A holds 2 balls, which he rolls simultaneously to goalkeeper B. Goalkeeper B picks up both balls and rolls them back to goalkeeper A, and so on.

• Handling the ball

Participants: 2 goalkeepers   **Equipment:** 1 or 2 balls

Starting position
The goalkeeper squats facing the coach, who stands 3 yards away holding a ball.

3 yds.

Phase 1
The coach throws the ball in an arc over the goalkeeper's head. The goalkeeper rolls backward and catches the ball, continuing the backward roll until his toes touch the ground.

Phase 2
The goalkeeper rolls forward again into the squatting position, throwing the ball back to the coach as he does so. The coach immediately throws the ball in an arc over the goalkeeper's head again, and so on.

Variation
A medicine ball is used instead of a soccer ball.

• Warming-up

Participants:	1 goalkeeper	Equipment:	1 ball
	Coach	Variation:	1 medicine ball

Key aspects
- General warming-up
- Take-off strength
- Catching the ball securely

Variations 2-5
- Agility
- Speed off the mark
- Leg extensor muscles

Variation 2
- Lower arm extensors
- Shoulder muscles

Starting position
The goalkeeper stands holding a ball.

Phase 1
The goalkeeper runs forward and throws the ball diagonally upward and forward.

Phase 2
The goalkeeper runs after the ball and jumps as high as possible to catch it in both hands. When he lands he immediately runs further and repeats the exercise, and so on.

Variations
1. The goalkeeper throws the ball up diagonally to the left or right.
2. The goalkeeper throws the ball 5 or 10 yards diagonally upward and forward. He then squats or sits, falls into the push-up position, lies face down or on his back or performs a forward or backward roll. He then springs to his feet as quickly as possible, sprints after the ball and jumps to catch it before it touches the ground.
3. The goalkeeper makes a complete clockwise or counter-clockwise turn or takes a stride in another direction before jumping to catch the ball.
4. The goalkeeper drops the ball and volleys it into the air.
5. The goalkeeper throws the ball into the air from a sitting position with legs together or legs apart or from a kneeling position.

● Warming-up

| Participant: 1 goalkeeper | Equipment: 1 ball |

Starting position
The goalkeeper and coach stand facing each other 5 yards apart. The coach is holding a ball.

Phase 1
The goalkeeper moves back and the coach moves forward so that they remain the same distance apart. As the coach moves forward he throws the ball low, medium-high and high to the goalkeeper. He continuously changes the height and direction of his throws.

Phase 2
As the goalkeeper moves back he gathers the ball or jumps up or dives to catch it. When he has the ball securely in both hands he throws it back to the coach and moves back again, and so on.

• Warming-up

31

Variations

1. The coach drops the ball and volleys it.

2. The coach lobs the ball over the goalkeeper who turns alternately clockwise or counter-clockwise and jumps to catch the ball as it falls.

3. The goalkeeper makes a complete clockwise or counter-clockwise turn as he moves back. As he turns the coach throws a low, medium-high or high ball, which the goalkeeper then blocks.

4. The above variations are carried out with the goalkeeper moving forward and the coach moving backward.

• **Warming-up**

| **Participants:** 1 goalkeeper Coach | **Equipment:** 1 ball |

Starting position
10 balls are distributed over an area measuring 10 x 10 yards. The goalkeeper and the coach stand beside each other among the balls.

Phase 1
The coach picks up the ball nearest to the goalkeeper and throws it into the air in front of the goalkeeper.

Phase 2
The goalkeeper jumps and catches the ball at the highest possible point. At the same time the coach picks up the next ball.

• **Warming-up**

Phase 3

As soon as the goalkeeper lands he puts the ball down and jumps to catch the next ball thrown by the coach, and so on.

The coach must throw the balls in such a way that the goalkeeper does not land on one of the balls on the ground.

Variations

1. The goalkeeper squats, sits, lies face down or on his back or performs a push-up or a forward roll or a backward roll or 2 consecutive forward rolls before jumping to catch the ball.

2. The goalkeeper performs a push-up and either a forward or a backward roll before jumping to catch the ball.

• Warming-up

Participants: 1 goalkeeper Coach	**Equipment:** 10 balls

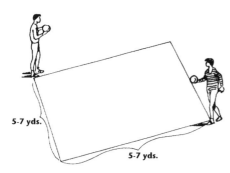

Starting position
The goalkeepers stand 5 to 7 yards apart at diagonally opposite corners of a rectangle with sides 5 to 7 yards long. Each of them is holding a ball.

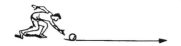

Phase 1
Each goalkeeper rolls his ball straight ahead.

Phase 2
Each goalkeeper moves to the side to get into line with the ball rolled by the other, then picks the ball up, and rolls it straight ahead again, and so on.

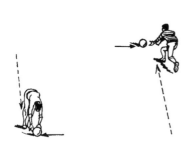

Variations
1. The goalkeepers throw the balls at medium-height so that they have to run and dive to catch them.
2. The goalkeepers lob the balls so that they have to run and jump to catch them.
3. The goalkeepers throw the balls randomly low, medium-high or high.

Participants: 2 goalkeepers   **Equipment:** 2 balls

• Warming-up

Key aspects
• General warming-up
• Reaction speed
• Catching the ball securely

Starting position
The goalkeepers stand facing each other 2 to 3 yards apart, each with one foot slightly ahead of the other. Each goalkeeper is holding a ball.

2-3 yds.

Phase 1
Each goalkeeper throws his ball to the other, taking care that the 2 balls do not collide.

Phase 2
Each goalkeeper catches the ball that is thrown to him and immediately throws it back, varying the height and direction of the throws.
The balls should be thrown rapidly, randomly varying the height and direction (low, high, to both sides and at the head of the receiving goalkeeper).

TEMPO !!

A   B

Variations
1. The distance between the 2 goalkeepers is reduced to 1 to 1.5 yards so that they have to react more quickly.
2. Goalkeeper A holds 2 balls and goalkeeper B holds 1. Goalkeeper A throws one ball at a time to goalkeeper B, who simultaneously throws his ball to A. The balls are thrown in rapid sequence.

• **Warming-up**

Participants: 2 goalkeepers	Equipment: 2 balls
	Variation 2: 3 balls

Starting position

10 balls are distributed over an area measuring 10 x 10 yards. The goalkeeper stands among the balls, with the coach behind him and to his right.

Phase 1

When the coach calls out, the goalkeeper runs to the nearest ball and lifts it to knee height.

Phase 2

The goalkeeper replaces the ball and sprints to the next ball, and so on. The goalkeeper must touch all of the balls in the shortest possible time.

Variations

After the goalkeeper replaces a ball the coach may call out, in which case the goalkeeper performs a forward roll, a jump-stride, a press-up or a stretching exercise.

· Warming-up

Participants: 1 goalkeeper Coach	**Equipment:** 10 balls

Starting position

The goalkeeper lies on his back with his legs stretched out straight. His eyes are directed to the ball, which he is holding diagonally behind his head with his arms straight.

Phase 1

The goalkeeper swings his straight right leg upward and tries to touch the ball with the tip of his foot while keeping his other leg on the ground.

Phase 2

The goalkeeper returns his right leg to the ground then repeats the movement with his left leg.

1.

2.

Variations

1. The goalkeeper lies on his right or left side.
2. The goalkeeper swings both legs upward to touch the ball.
The goalkeeper sits up quickly and touches his toes with the ball while his legs remain straight.

• Abdominal muscles

Participant: 1 goalkeeper	**Equipment:** 1 ball

Starting position

The goalkeeper lies on his back with his legs straight and slightly apart. The coach stands about 1 yard from his feet, holding a ball.

Phase 1

The coach throws the ball forward and the goalkeeper sits up and catches it.

Phase 2

The goalkeeper immediately throws the ball back to the coach and lies back on the ground again. The coach throws the ball to him again, and so on.

• Abdominal muscles

39

3.

Variations

1. Use a medicine ball instead of a soccer ball.

2. The coach throws the ball alternately to the right and left of the goalkeeper.

3. The goalkeeper lies on his side with his body at an angle to his legs, so that his feet and arms point towards the coach. The coach throws the ball and the goalkeeper sits up and catches it, then lies on his other side.

• Abdominal muscles

Abdominal muscles •

Starting position

The goalkeeper lies on his back with his legs slightly apart. The coach sits on the goalkeeper's lower legs and ankles and presses down lightly on his thighs, so that he cannot bend his knees. A ball is placed on each side of the goalkeeper, which he can just reach by raising his upper body and leaning to the side.

Phase 1

The goalkeeper raises his upper body and bends to the right to grasp the ball with both hands (first ball).

Phase 2

The goalkeeper lies back on the ground and places the ball at the full stretch of his arms in a straight line behind his head.

Phase 3

The goalkeeper raises his upper body and bends to the left to grasp the ball with both hands (second ball).

Phase 4
The goalkeeper, keeping his arms straight, takes the ball through an arc behind his head, over the first ball, and finally places it to his right, where the first ball was initially positioned.

Phase 5
The goalkeeper stretches his arms backward and picks up the first ball, then raises his upper body and places the ball to his left. He then starts the cycle with phase 1 again, and so on.

Variation
1. Use 2 medicine balls instead of soccer balls.

• Abdominal muscles

Participants: 1 goalkeeper		**Equipment:**	1 ball
Coach ,		**Variation:**	2 medicine balls

Starting position

The goalkeeper lies face down with his eyes directed toward the coach, who stands 2 yards in front of him holding a ball. The goalkeeper's arms are stretched out straight toward the coach.

Phase 1

The coach throws the ball medium-high to the goalkeeper. The goalkeeper raises his upper body, stretches his arms toward the ball and catches it in front of his head.

Phase 2

The goalkeeper immediately throws the ball back to the coach and lies back on the ground again. The coach throws the ball to him again, and so on.

• **Back muscles**

4.

Variations
1. Use a medicine ball instead of a soccer ball.
2. The coach throws the ball alternately to the right and left of the goalkeeper.
3. After catching the ball the goalkeeper rolls away to the right or left before throwing the ball back to the coach.
4. The coach rolls the ball at random to the right or left of the goalkeeper, who twists and grasps it with both hands.
5. A second goalkeeper kneels behind the active goalkeeper and holds his lower legs firmly against the ground. The goalkeepers swap roles after a suitable period.

• **Back muscles**

Participants: 1 goalkeeper
          Coach

Equipment: 1 ball
Variation 1-5: 1 medicine ball

Starting position

The goalkeeper lies in the press-up position facing the coach, who is 3 yards away and is holding a ball.

Phase 1

The coach throws the ball alternately to left or right at the goalkeeper's elbow height.

Phase 2

The goalkeeper lifts one hand off the ground and catches the ball, then throws it back to the coach, and so on.

Variations

When the goalkeeper catches the ball, he takes it behind and across the other arm before throwing it back to the coach.

• Arm muscles

Participants: 1 goalkeeper Coach	Equipment: 1 ball

Starting position
The goalkeeper lies on his back, with his hands pressing against the ground at his sides and his legs held straight at an angle of 45 degrees to the ground. The coach leans his upper body and hands against the ball, which he presses against the goalkeeper's feet.

Phase 1
The goalkeeper pulls his legs back and bends his knees as far as possible while the coach presses the ball hard against his feet.

Phase 2
The goalkeeper stretches his legs against the resistance of the coach, who presses all of his body weight against the ball.

Variations
1. The coach stands 3 yards away from the goalkeeper, who lies on his back on the ground with his feet pointing toward the coach. The coach lobs the ball up into the air. The goalkeeper pulls his legs back and bends his knees, then stretches his legs to meet the ball with the soles of his feet and tap it back into the coach's hands.
2. Use a medicine ball instead of a soccer ball.

● Leg muscles

Participants:	1 goalkeeper	Equipment:	1 ball
	Coach	Variation 2:	1 medicine ball

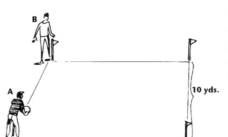

Starting position

A square measuring 10 yards by 10 yards is marked by flags at each corner. A goalkeeper stands beside each flag on one side of the square. Goalkeeper A holds a medicine ball.

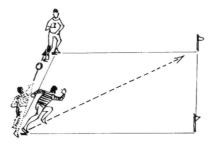

Phase 1

Holding the ball on the palm of one hand at shoulder height, goalkeeper A launches it powerfully toward goalkeeper B and sprints to the diagonally opposite corner of the square.

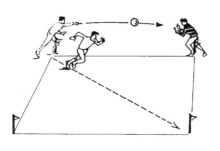

Phase 2

Goalkeeper B uses both hands to catch the medicine ball. He waits until goalkeeper A is ready in his new position and facing him again, then launches the ball toward goalkeeper A and sprints to the diagonally opposite corner. And so on.

• Speed off the mark

Variations

1. The goalkeeper holding the medicine ball uses the throw-in technique to toss the ball to the other goalkeeper at waist or chest height.

2. The goalkeeper with the medicine ball holds it with both hands in front of his chest (elbows at shoulder height, pointing outward) before straightening his arms and launching the ball hard toward the other goalkeeper. To apply maximum force, he leans his upper body back and pushes his hips forward.

• Speed off the mark

| Participants: 2 goalkeepers | Equipment: | 1 medicine ball |
| | | 4 marker flags |

Key aspects
- Catching technique
- Picking up a low ball
- Reaction speed
- Catching the ball securely

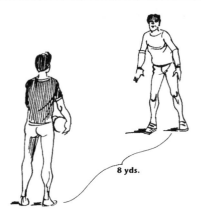

Starting position
The goalkeeper stands facing the coach, who is 8 yards away and is holding a ball.

8 yds.

Phase 1
The coach drops the ball and half-volleys it low to the goalkeeper, varying the speed and direction of the ball each time.

Phase 2
The goalkeeper moves to the side or moves forward to gather the ball. He must position his fingers correctly and secure the ball properly after picking it up. He throws the ball back into the coach's hands and then resumes his starting position, so that the coach can immediately kick the ball to him again, and so on.

Participants: 1 goalkeeper
Coach

Equipment: 1 ball

Key aspects
- Catching technique
- Agility
- Diving to stop low shots
- Diving to stop high to medium-high shots
- Rolling away to the side

- Take-off strength
- Reaction speed
- Catching the ball securely

Variation 2
- 2-fisted punching

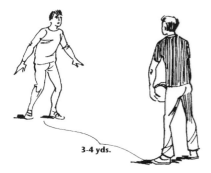

Starting position
The goalkeeper stands facing the coach, who is 3 to 4 yards away and is holding a ball.

Phase 1
The coach drops the ball and half-volleys it hard at the goalkeeper, varying the height and direction of the ball each time.

3-4 yds.

Phase 2
The goalkeeper must gather the ball or dive and catch it. The shots can come at him at all heights and be directed at his body or to his right or left. He must use the correct catching technique and secure the ball properly after catching it. He throws the ball back into the coach's hands and then resumes his starting position, so that the coach can immediately kick the ball to him again, and so on.

Variations
1. The goalkeeper kneels instead of standing, so the coach has to take care not to kick the ball too high or too wide of him.
2. The coach kicks the ball straight at the goalkeeper and the goalkeeper punches it away with both fists.

• Catching technique

Participants: 1 goalkeeper
Coach

Equipment: 1 ball
Variation 2: 5 balls

Key aspects
- Catching technique
- Rolling away to the side
- Reaction speed
- Catching the ball securely

Starting position
The goalkeeper kneels facing the coach, who is 5 yards away and has a ball at his feet.

5 yds.

Phase 1
The coach kicks the ball randomly along the ground to the left and right of the goalkeeper.

Phase 2
The goalkeeper falls to the side and grabs the ball with both hands and clutches it securely to his body. While still lying on the ground he throws the ball back to the coach and then kneels again, and so on.

Variations
The goalkeeper squats instead of kneeling.

Participants: 1 goalkeeper
Coach

Equipment: 1 ball

Key aspects
- Catching technique
- Agility
- Diving to stop low shots
- Diving to stop high to medium-high shots

- Take-off strength
- Catching the ball securely

Variation
- Reaction speed

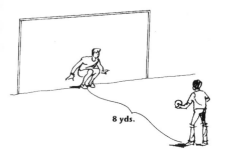

Starting position
The goalkeeper squats on the goal line in the middle of the goal, facing the coach, who stands 8 yards in front of the goal, holding a ball.

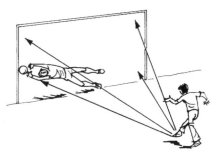

Phase 1
The coach drops the ball and shoots low, medium-high or high just inside either post. The goalkeeper dives toward the ball.

Phase 2
The goalkeeper catches the ball, taking care to use the correct catching technique, and immediately clutches the ball securely to his body. After landing he throws the ball back into the coach's hands and then resumes his starting position, so that the coach can immediately shoot again, and so on.

Variations
The coach shoots at random inside the right and left posts.

• Catching technique

Participants: 1 goalkeeper Coach	**Equipment:** 1 ball 1 goal

Key aspects
- Agility
- Diving to stop high to medium-high shots
- Take-off strength
- Catching technique
- Speed off the mark
- Leg extensors
- Trunk muscles
- Arm muscles

Starting position
The goalkeeper stands holding a ball.

Phase 1
The goalkeeper throws the ball up and back over his head.

Phase 2
Immediately after throwing the ball the goalkeeper performs a backward roll.

Phase 3
As he comes out of the backward roll the goalkeeper turns toward the ball and dives to catch it in both hands before it touches the ground. He resumes his starting position, and so on.

• Agility

Variations

1. The goalkeeper throws the ball diagonally upward and forward and performs a forward roll.

2. The goalkeeper holds the ball above his head in both hands and bounces it hard against the ground before he performs a forward roll.

3. After the goalkeeper bounces the ball he turns through 180 degrees and performs a backward roll. As he comes out of the roll he turns toward the ball.

• Agility

Participant: 1 goalkeeper   **Equipment:** 1 ball

Starting position

The goalkeeper stands on the 18-yard line facing the middle of the goal. He is holding a ball. Another ball lies at the corner of the goal area.

Phase 1

The goalkeeper rolls the ball towards the goal at a speed that will allow him to overtake it before it crosses the goal line. As he releases the ball he sprints toward the ball at the corner of the goal area.

Phase 2

The goalkeeper dives to grasp the ball at the corner of the goal area and clasps it securely to his chest, then replaces it in its original position.

• Agility

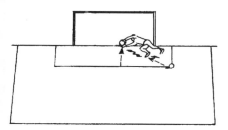

Phase 3

The goalkeeper turns and sprints toward the rolling ball. He dives at the ball and tries to grab it or deflect it before it crosses the line. He then returns to his starting position with this ball, and so on.

Variations

1. The goalkeeper touches the ball at the corner of the goal area with one hand, turns toward the goal, performs a forward roll and as he comes out of the roll he dives forward onto the rolling ball.

2. The coach stands to the left (or right) of the goalkeeper on the edge of the penalty area. He has a ball at his feet and 5 balls to his left or right. At a signal from the coach the goalkeeper sprints to the ball at the left (or right) corner of the goal area. As soon as the goalkeeper touches this ball, the coach sidefoots a ball along the ground toward the left (or right) corner of the goal. The coach gradually kicks the ball harder, but the goalkeeper must always have a chance of reaching it.

3. The coach bounces the ball toward the corner of the goal.

• Agility

Participant:	1 goalkeeper	Equipment:	2 balls
Variations 2 and 3:	Coach		1 goal
			Penalty area
		Variations 2 and 3:	7 balls

Key aspects
- Agility
- Diving to stop low shots
- Take-off strength
- Catching the ball securely
- Throwing the ball into play
- Speed off the mark
- Trunk muscles
- Arm muscles

Variations
- Leg extensors
- Shoulder muscles

Starting position
The goalkeeper stands holding a ball.

Phase 1
The goalkeeper rolls the ball forward.

Phase 2
The goalkeeper performs a forward roll.

Phase 3
The goalkeeper runs after the ball, dives on it and clutches it securely to his body. He then stands up and starts at phase 1 again.

Variations
After rolling the ball forward the goal keeper turns through 360 degrees o performs a backward roll, or squats o sits, or falls into the push-up position o lies face down or on his back.

• Agility

Participant: 1 goalkeeper	Equipment: 1 ball

Key aspects
- Agility
- Diving to stop low and medium-high shots
- Take-off strength

- Reaction speed
- Catching the ball securely
- Deflecting the ball

Variations
- Lower arm extensors
- Shoulder muscles

Starting position
The goalkeeper is in the push-up position. The coach stands 3 yards away, opposite to the goalkeeper's feet, and holds a ball. Five other balls are on the ground at the coach's feet.

Phase 1
The goalkeeper performs push-ups. When the coach calls out, the goalkeeper immediately turns toward the coach.

Phase 2
When the goalkeeper turns toward him, the coach throws the ball medium-high or low about 1 yard away from the goalkeeper's feet. The goalkeeper dives toward the ball and catches or deflects it. He throws the ball back to the coach after catching it. The goalkeeper then resumes the press-up position.

Variations
The coach stands facing the goalkeeper from a distance of 3 yards. The goalkeeper performs press-ups and watches the coach, who throws the ball medium-high or low about 1.5 yards away from the goalkeeper's feet. The goalkeeper pushes himself up from the ground with his hands and dives toward the ball.

• Agility

Participants: 1 goalkeeper
Coach

Equipment: 6 balls

3 yds.

Starting position
The goalkeeper lies on his side facing the coach. He holds his upper body off the ground with both arms, while his hip and thigh touch the ground. The coach stands 3 yards away, level with his feet, and holds a ball.

Phase 1
While the goalkeeper pushes himself up from the ground with both hands, the coach throws the ball medium-high beyond the goalkeeper's feet.

Phase 2
The goalkeeper continues his upward movement by diving to catch the ball. When he lands he immediately throws the ball back to the coach and resumes his starting position, and so on.

• **Agility**

Variations
1. The coach throws the ball alternately to right and left.
2. The coach gradually increases the height of the throw.
3. The coach throws the ball to one side of the goalkeeper's head. The goalkeeper pushes himself up off the ground and dives to catch the ball
4. The goalkeeper pushes himself off the ground without using his hands.
5. The coach shoots 1 to 1.5 yards to the side of the goalkeeper's head. As the coach takes his final step before shooting, the goalkeeper pushes himself off the ground so that he can dive to catch the shot.

• Agility

Participants: 1 goalkeeper
Coach

Equipment: 1 ball

Key aspects
- Agility
- Diving to stop low shots
- Diving to stop high to medium-high shots
- Take-off strength

- Reaction speed
- Catching the ball securely
- Lower arm extensors
- Shoulder muscles

Starting position

The goalkeeper stands facing the coach, who is standing 3 yards away and is holding a ball.

3 yds.

1 – 3 ×

Phase 1

The goalkeeper performs 1 to 3 push-ups.

Phase 2

When the coach calls out, the goalkeeper adopts a squatting position and dives to catch the ball, which the coach throws randomly low, medium-high or high to his right or left.

Phase 3

While on the ground, the goalkeeper throws the ball back to the coach. The goalkeeper then returns to the push-up position, and so on.

• **Agility**

Participants: 1 goalkeeper	Equipment: 1 ball
Coach	

Key aspects
- Agility
- Diving to stop low shots
- Diving to stop high to medium-high shots
- Take-off strength
- Reaction speed
- Catching the ball securely

Starting position
The goalkeeper kneels facing the coach, who is standing 3 yards away and is holding a ball.

Phase 1
The coach throws the ball hard and low, high or medium-high to the right or left of the goalkeeper. The goalkeeper dives toward the ball and must bring it securely under control.

Phase 2
While on the ground, the goalkeeper throws the ball back to the coach. The goalkeeper then returns to the kneeling position, and so on.

• Agility

Participants: 1 goalkeeper
Coach

Equipment: 1 ball

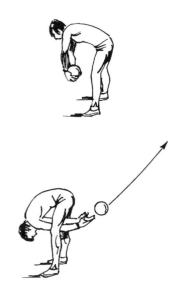

Starting position

The goalkeeper stands with legs wide apart and his body bent forward and his arms hanging down holding a ball at knee height.

Phase 1

The goalkeeper throws the ball back high to medium-high between his legs. Initially, to make things easier, he can throw the ball back and to the side to which he is going to turn.

Phase 2

The goalkeeper immediately turns and dives to catch the ball before it falls to the ground, and so on.

Variations

1. The goalkeeper throws the ball alternately to right and left.

2. To increase the distance that he must dive, the goalkeeper turns counterclockwise when he throws the ball to the right and clockwise when he throws the ball to the left.

3. The goalkeeper throws the ball back high, so that he can catch it as he jumps upward.

4. The goalkeeper rolls the ball backward so that he can run and dive to gather it.

• Agility

Participant: 1 goalkeeper	Equipment: 1 ball

Starting position
The goalkeeper sits on the ground with his legs bent, supporting himself with his arms to the side. He faces the coach, who stands 3 yards away, holding a ball.

Phase 1
The coach throws the ball in an arc over the goalkeeper's head, so that it drops behind the goalkeeper. The goalkeeper pushes himself up and dives to catch the ball.

Phase 2
The goalkeeper catches the ball in both hands, and on landing he throws the ball back immediately to the coach.

Phase 3
The coach catches the ball and the goalkeeper returns to the sitting position. The coach then throws the ball over the goalkeeper's head again, and so on.

Variations
The coach throws the ball in an arc so that it comes down to the right or left of the goalkeeper.

• Agility

Participants: 1 goalkeeper
Coach

Equipment: 1 ball

64

Starting position
The goalkeeper squats facing the coach, who is standing 3 yards away and is holding a ball.

Phase 1
The coach throws the ball high to medium-high to the goalkeeper's right. The goalkeeper dives to catch the ball.

Phase 2
When the goalkeeper lands he throws the ball back immediately to the coach.

Agility

Phase 3

The coach catches the ball and the goal-keeper returns to the squatting position. The coach throws the ball high to medium-high to the goalkeeper's left, and so on.

Variations

1. The coach throws the ball several times in succession to the same side before switching to the other side.

2. The coach throws the ball high to medium-high to the goalkeeper's right, then along the ground to his left, and vice versa.

3. The coach throws the ball alternately to the goalkeeper's right or left, varying the height (low or high to medium-high) at random.

• Agility

Participants: 1 goalkeeper
Coach

Equipment: 1 ball

Key aspects
• Agility
• Diving to stop high to medium-high shots
• Take-off strength
• Reaction speed
• Catching the ball securely

Starting position

The goalkeeper lies face down on the ground with his head toward the coach, who stands 3 yards away holding a ball.

Phase 1

The coach throws the ball upward to the right or left of the goalkeeper. The goalkeeper pushes himself up and dives or jumps to catch the ball.

Phase 2

The goalkeeper catches the ball, throws it back to the coach and resumes his starting position, and so on.

Variations

The goalkeeper lies on his back with his feet pointing toward the coach.

• Agility

Participants: 1 goalkeeper	Equipment: 1 ball
Coach	

Key aspects
- Agility
- Diving to stop low shots
- Diving to stop medium-high shots
- Take-off strength
- Reaction speed
- Catching the ball securely

Starting position
The goalkeeper lies face down on the ground with his head toward the coach, who stands 4 yards away holding a ball.

Phase 1
The coach bounces the ball to the right or left of the goalkeeper or straight at him. He continuously varies the direction, speed and height of the ball.

Phase 2
The goalkeeper dives toward the ball and tries to catch it in both hands and clutch it securely to his body. He throws the ball back to the coach and returns to his starting position, and so on.

Variations
1. The goalkeeper dives from a squatting position.
2. The goalkeeper dives from a standing position.

• **Agility**

Participants: 1 goalkeeper
Coach

Equipment: 1 ball

Key aspects
- Agility
- Diving to stop low shots
- Diving to stop high to medium-high shots
- Rolling away to the side
- Take-off strength
- Reaction speed
- Catching the ball securely
- Leg extensors
- Trunk muscles
- Arm muscles

Starting position
The goalkeeper, holding a ball, stands facing the coach, who stands 5 yards away.

Phase 1
The goalkeeper rolls the ball to the coach. After releasing the ball he performs a forward roll.

• Agility

Phase 2

The coach shoots high, medium-high or low at the goalkeeper, continuously varying the direction and strength of the shot. As the goalkeeper comes out of his forward roll he dives to catch the ball securely in both hands. He then stands facing the coach and rolls the ball to him, and so on.

3.

Variations

1. The goalkeeper performs a backward roll.

2. The distance between goalkeeper and coach is extended to 7 yards. The goalkeeper carries out 2 forward rolls in succession.

3. The coach holds the ball. The goalkeeper performs a forward roll over 2 balls standing in line. As he comes out of the forward roll he dives to catch the ball, which the coach has thrown low to the side.

4. The goalkeeper lies face down with his arms stretched out straight along the ground, pointing toward the coach, who stands 5 yards away. The goalkeeper watches the coach. At a call from the coach the goalkeeper performs a forward roll and dives to catch the ball, which the coach can throw at random.

• Agility

Participants: 1 goalkeeper	Equipment: 1 ball
Coach	Variation 3: 3 balls

Key aspects
- Agility
- Diving to stop low shots
- Diving to stop high to medium-high shots
- Take-off strength
- Reaction speed
- Catching the ball securely
- Deflecting the ball

Variation 3
- Leg extensors
- Arm muscles

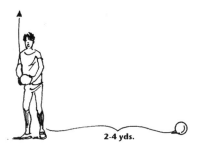

Starting position
The goalkeeper stands holding a ball. Another ball lies on the ground 2 to 4 yards to his left.

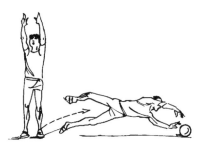

Phase 1
The goalkeeper throws the ball that he is holding straight up into the air in front of his body and dives to the ball on the ground to his left.

Phase 2
After the goalkeeper has touched the ball on the ground with both hands, he springs to his feet, turns and dives toward the falling ball, trying to catch it before it touches the ground. If he does not achieve this he should block it on the first bounce.

• Agility

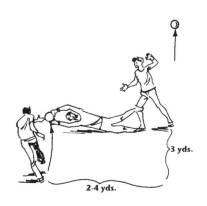

3 yds.

2-4 yds.

Variations

1. The coach stands 3 yards in front and 2 to 4 yards to the side of the goalkeeper. When the goalkeeper throws his ball into the air, the coach hit a low shot with the second ball, which the goalkeeper must stop.

2. The coach throws the second ball high to medium-high instead of kicking it.

3. The goalkeeper adopts a squatting rather than a standing position and throws a medicine ball into the air.

• Agility

Participant:	1 goalkeeper	**Equipment:**	2 balls
Variations 1 and 2:	1 goalkeeper	**Variation 3:**	1 ball
	Coach		1 medicine ball

Starting position

The goalkeeper squats in the middle of a 10 yd X 7 yd rectangle. On each corner is a marker flag. The goalkeeper faces the coach, who is standing 4.5 yards away in line with two of the markers. The coach holds a ball and there are 5 balls on the ground nearby.

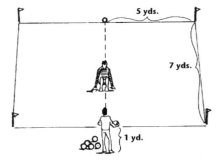

Phase 1

The coach throws the ball alternately into the zones to right and left of the goalkeeper at different speeds and heights. The squatting goalkeeper dives to catch the ball in flight.

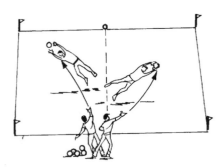

• Agility

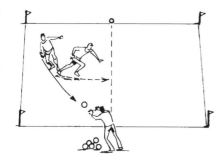

Phase 2

The goalkeeper throws the ball back to the coach and sprints back to the goal line. As soon as he reaches his starting position, the coach throws the next ball into the other zone.

Variations

1. The coach throws the balls randomly into the 2 zones.

2. The coach throws the ball into the 2 zones so that the goalkeeper can only just reach them. If the goalkeeper does not manage to catch the ball, he must try to deflect or punch it out of the zone. The ball should not be allowed to touch the ground.

• **Agility**

| **Participants:** 1 goalkeeper | **Equipment:** 8 balls |
| Coach | 4 marker flags |

Starting position

Two marker flags represent the posts of a goal 7 yards wide. A third marker flag is placed 3 yards behind the center point of the goal line, creating 2 more goals of equal width. The goalkeeper stands in the triangle between the 3 goals and faces the coach, who stands holding a ball 5 yards away from the front goal. There are another 5 balls on the ground nearby.

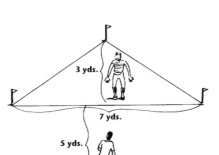

Phase 1

The coach randomly throws the ball low, medium-high or high, or lobs it at the front goal. The goalkeeper must stop the ball before it crosses the goal line. If he fails to do this, he must stop the ball before it crosses the goal line of the left goal or the right goal. He can catch the ball, punch it or deflect it. When he catches the ball he rolls it back to the coach.

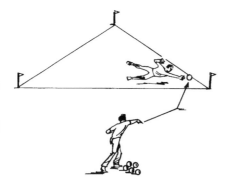

• Agility

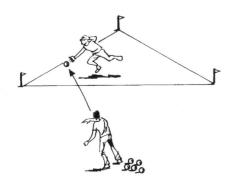

Phase 2

As the goalkeeper sprints back to his starting position, the coach picks up the next ball and throws it. He can throw it towards the left or the right goal. The running goalkeeper dives to stop the ball, preferably before it crosses the front goal line, but if this is not possible then before it crosses the line of the right or the left goal. And so on.

Variations

1. The coach stands 10 yards from the front goal line and shoots hard at goal rather than throwing the balls.
2. The coach drops the balls and half-volleys them.

• Agility

| Participants: 1 goalkeeper | Equipment: 6 balls |
| Coach | 3 marker flags |

Starting position

The goalkeeper stands beside one of the goalposts facing the coach, who stands holding a ball 7 yards in front of the goal. There are another 5 balls on the ground nearby.

7 yds.

Phase 1

The goalkeeper crawls on all fours toward the other goalpost. The coach calls out and throws the ball to the side of the goal that the goalkeeper is heading for. The coach throws the ball at different heights and speeds.

• Agility

Phase 2

When the coach calls out, the goalkeeper springs to his feet and dives to stop the ball. If possible he should catch it with both hands. If not, he can deflect it over the bar or round the post or punch it away. After catching the ball the goalkeeper rolls it back to the coach and immediately starts to crawl back along the goal line in the reverse direction. The coach picks up the next ball, and so on.

Variations

1. The goalkeeper squats on the goal line and waddles or hops along it or performs 2 forward rolls.

2. The coach does not call out until the goalkeeper has covered half of the goal line. The coach then throws the ball toward the side of the goal behind the goalkeeper. The goalkeeper has to turn quickly to dive and stop the ball.

3. The goalkeeper stands in front of one of the goalposts. The coach throws the ball toward the other side of the goal. The goalkeeper runs and dives to stop the ball.

4. The coach lets the ball fall and half-volleys it powerfully at goal from the edge of the penalty area.

● **Agility**

Participants: 1 goalkeeper	**Equipment:** 6 balls
Coach	1 goal

Key aspects
- Agility
- Diving to stop low shots
- Diving to stop high to medium-
  high shots
- Take-off strength
- Reaction speed
- Catching the ball securely

Variations 2-4
- Punching the ball
- Deflecting the ball

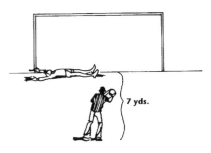

Starting position
The goalkeeper lies on his back beside his right goalpost. His arms are stretched straight out behind his head, pointing toward the goalpost. The coach stands 7 yards in front of the center of the goal and holds a ball.

7 yds.

Phase 1
At a call from the coach, the goalkeeper springs to his feet and dives to the other side of the goal to catch the ball thrown by the coach.

Phase 2
The goalkeeper throws the ball back to the coach and then lies on his back beside his left goalpost. The coach catches the ball and waits until the goalkeeper is in position on the ground, and so on.

• Agility

79

Variations
1. The goalkeeper lies on his back with his feet pointing toward the goalpost.
2. The coach throws the ball so close to the other goalpost that the goalkeeper can only deflect or punch it over the bar or round the post. For these variations the coach needs 10 balls, which lie on the ground nearby.
3. The coach stands on the penalty spot with 10 balls on the ground nearby. When the goalkeeper jumps to his feet and looks at him, he shoots at the other corner of the goal.
4. The coach waits until the goalkeeper has passed the middle of the goal, then throws the ball toward the side of the goal behind him. The goalkeeper must turn quickly and dive to stop the ball.

4.

11 yds.

• Agility

Participants:	1 goalkeeper	Equipment:	1 ball
	Coach		1 goal
		Variation 2 and 4:	10 balls

Starting position

One ball lies on the goal line 1 to 2 yards from one goalpost, while the goalkeeper stands on the goal line halfway between the ball and the other goalpost. The coach holds 1 ball and there are another 4 on the ground beside him. He stands 5 yards in front of the side of the goal into which he will throw the balls.

Phase 1

When the coach calls out, the goalkeeper sprints to the ball on the goal line and touches it.

Phase 2

When the goalkeeper has touched the ball he turns toward the coach, who immediately throws a ball low, medium-high or high toward the other side of the goal. The goalkeeper dives to catch, deflect or punch the ball. And so on.

• Agility

81

Variations

1. The coach stands 10 to 12 yards in front of the goal and shoots low, medium-high or high toward the side of the goal, gradually increasing the power of the shots.

2. The goalkeeper dives at the ball on the goal line and clasps it securely to his body. He replaces it, turns to the coach and tries to stop the ball flying toward the other side of the goal.

3. The ball on the goal line is removed. The goalkeeper has to touch the goalpost and then start back toward the other side of the goal to dive and stop the ball thrown by the coach.

4. After the goalkeeper has touched the goalpost, he makes a running dive onto a ball positioned on the edge of the goal area, 1 yard to the right of the center of the goal. The goalkeeper clasps the ball securely to his body and then replaces it. The coach, who stands 8 yards from the goal line in front of the left corner, then throws the next ball toward the left goalpost.

• Agility

Participants: 1 goalkeeper	**Equipment:**	6 balls
Coach		1 goal
	Variation 4:	1 goal area

Key aspects
- Agility
- Diving to stop high to medium-high shots
- Take-off strength (running take-off from one foot)
- Catching the ball securely
- Kicking the ball into play
- Speed off the mark

Variation 2
- Leg extensors
- Hip muscles
- Trunk muscles
- Arm muscles

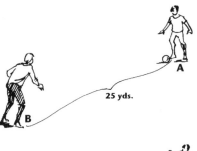

25 yds.

Starting position
Two goalkeepers stand facing each other 25 yards apart. Goalkeeper A has a ball at his feet.

Phase 1
Goalkeeper A kicks the ball medium-high toward goalkeeper B. Goalkeeper B sprints to meet the ball and dives forward to catch it before it touches the ground.

20 yds.

Phase 2
Goalkeeper B sprints back to his starting position with the ball. He places it on the ground and kicks it medium-high toward goalkeeper A, and so on.

1.

Variations
1. The distance between the goalkeepers is reduced to 10 yards. Goalkeeper A holds the ball above his head and bounces it powerfully toward goalkeeper B. Goalkeeper B sprints to meet the ball and dives forward to catch it before it touches the ground.
2. Goalkeeper B turns through 360 degrees or performs a forward roll before sprinting to meet the ball, or lies face down on the ground or in the press-up position or sits with his legs apart before springing to his feet and sprinting to meet the ball.

• **Agility**

Participants: 2 goalkeepers   **Equipment:** 1 ball

Starting position
Goalkeepers A and B stand facing each other 15 yards apart. Each of them holds a ball.

Phase 1
Each goalkeeper holds the ball in one hand with his fingers pointing upward. They throw the balls simultaneously to each other. Goalkeeper A throws the ball low, medium-high or high to either side of goalkeeper B, while goalkeeper B throws the ball up into the air.

Phase 2
Goalkeeper A jumps to catch the ball, while goalkeeper B rolls away or dives to the side. Each goalkeeper grasps the ball securely in both hands and goes back to his starting position, and so on.
After 5 throws the goalkeepers switch positions.

Variations
Each goalkeeper throws the ball low, medium-high or high to either side of or directly at the other. After each throw they sprint to switch positions.

• Agility

Participants: 2 goalkeepers   **Equipment:** 2 balls

- Agility
- Take-off strength
  (running take-off from one foot)
- Catching the ball securely
- Throwing the ball into play
- Speed off the mark
- Leg muscles

Variations 1 and 2
- Diving to stop high to medium-
  high shots

Variation 2
- Trunk muscles
- Arm muscles

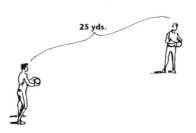

25 yds.

Starting position
The 2 goalkeepers stand facing each other 25 yards apart. Each of them holds a ball.

Phase 1
The goalkeepers throw the balls overarm toward each other so that they bounce about half way between them.

Phase 2
The goalkeepers sprint toward each other. Each takes off from one foot and catches the ball thrown by the other.

• Agility

Phase 3
After catching the ball each goalkeeper drops into a squatting position and moves quickly to the other's starting position, where he stands up again.

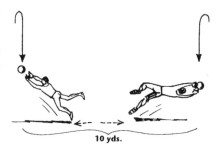

10 yds.

Variations
1. The goalkeepers stand 10 yards apart. Each throws the ball 2-handed vertically into the air and then immediately sprints forward to dive and catch the other's ball before it touches the ground.
2. After throwing the ball, each goalkeeper performs a forward roll, sprints forward and dives to catch the other's ball before it can bounce twice.

• Agility

Participants: 2 goalkeepers	Equipment: 2 balls

Key aspects
- Agility
- Catching the ball securely
- Hip flexors
- Trunk muscles

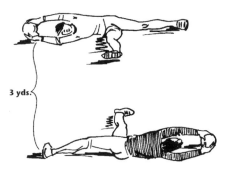

3 yds.

Starting position
The goalkeepers lie on their right side facing each other at a distance of 3 yards. Each holds a ball above his head with his arms straight, while his right leg points at the other goalkeeper and his left leg is in line with his body.

Phase 1
The goalkeepers throw the balls forward at medium height so that they can be caught with both hands. As each goalkeeper throws the ball he pushes his upper body off the ground and to the left and lies on his left side, with his right leg pointing at the other goalkeeper and his left leg in line with his body.

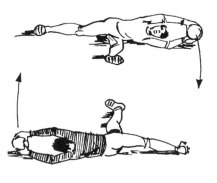

Phase 2
As each goalkeeper lies on his left side he catches the ball thrown by the other before it touches the ground. They then throw the ball again, and so on.

Agility

Participants: 2 goalkeepers	Equipment: 2 balls

Key aspects
- Agility
- Diving to stop high to medium-high shots
- Take-off strength
- Reaction speed
- Catching the ball securely

- Trunk muscles
- Arm muscles

Variations 1 and 2
- Catching the ball when diving forward

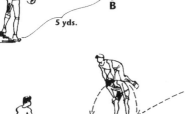

Starting position
Goalkeeper B bends over 3 yards in front of goalkeeper A. The coach stands facing goalkeeper B at a distance of 5 yards. The coach is holding a ball.

Phase 1
Goalkeeper A jumps over goalkeeper B.

Phase 2
On landing, goalkeeper A performs a forward roll. At the same time goalkeeper B stands up straight.

Phase 3
As soon as goalkeeper A springs to his feet after coming out of the forward roll the coach throws the ball low or at medium height to his right or left. The goalkeeper dives to catch the ball and clasps it safely to his body. Goalkeeper A throws the ball back to the coach and goes back to his starting position behind goalkeeper B, and so on.
After 5 cycles the goalkeepers swap tasks.

Variations
1. The coach bounces the ball or lobs it into the air toward goalkeeper A.
2. After the jump, goalkeeper A turns through 360 degrees.

• **Agility**

Participants: 2 goalkeepers
Coach

Equipment: 1 ball

Key aspects

- Agility
- Diving to stop high to medium-high shots
- Take-off strength
- Catching the ball securely
- Trunk muscles
- Arm muscles

Variations

- Leg extensors
- Hip muscles

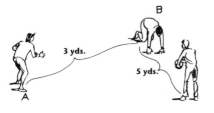

Starting position

Goalkeeper A stands 3 yards from goal-keeper B, who is kneeling on all fours with his right side towards goalkeeper A. The coach stands facing goalkeeper B at a distance of 5 yards. He holds a ball.

Phase 1

Goalkeeper A performs a forward roll. When he comes out of the forward roll he creeps along the ground toward goalkeeper B.

Phase 2

Goalkeeper B straightens his knees, creating sufficient clearance for goalkeeper A to crawl under him.

Phase 3

Goalkeeper B returns to his starting posi-tion. As goalkeeper A stands up, he turns to face the coach, who throws the ball 1 or 2 yards to the right of goalkeeper A.

Phase 4

Goalkeeper A dives over the kneeling goalkeeper B and catches the ball with both hands. After landing he throws the ball back to the coach and resumes his starting position again, and so on.

After 5 cycles the goalkeepers swap roles.

Variations

Instead of performing a forward roll, the goalkeeper can perform a press-up, take steps to the right or left, turn clockwise or counter-clockwise through 360 degrees, lie face down or on his back, etc.

• **Agility**

Participants: 2 goalkeepers
Coach

Equipment: 1 ball

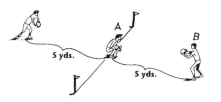

Starting position
Goalkeeper A squats in the middle of a goal formed by 2 marker flags. The coach stands 5 yards behind him and goalkeeper B stands 5 yards in front of him. Both the coach and goalkeeper B are holding a ball.

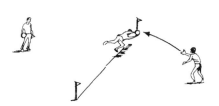

Phase 1
Goalkeeper B throws the ball to goalkeeper A's left. Goalkeeper A dives to catch the ball with both hands.

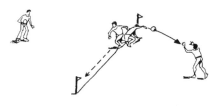

Phase 2
As he lies on the ground, goalkeeper A throws the ball back to goalkeeper B. As goalkeeper A springs to his feet, he turns and looks at the coach and runs back to the middle of the goal.

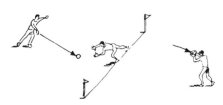

Phase 3
The coach throws the ball to goalkeeper A's left. At the same time goalkeeper B catches the ball that goalkeeper A threw back to him.

• Agility

91

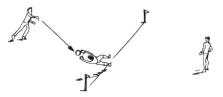

Phase 4
Goalkeeper A runs to his left and dives to catch the ball thrown by the coach in both hands.

Phase 5
After landing, goalkeeper A throws the ball back to the coach, turns and runs back to the middle of the goal. The coach picks the ball up. Everyone is now in the original starting position again. However, goalkeeper A does not adopt a squatting position but runs and dives to catch the ball thrown by goalkeeper B, and so on.

After 5 cycles the goalkeepers swap roles.

Variations
1. The coach and goalkeeper B take turns in throwing the ball low to goalkeeper A.

2. The coach and goalkeeper B take turns in throwing the ball high to medium-high to goalkeeper A.

3. The coach and goalkeeper B still take turns but throw the ball randomly low, medium-high or high to goalkeeper A.

4. The coach and goalkeeper B throw the balls very hard.

5. The coach and goalkeeper B stand 10 yards from the goal line and shoot rather than throw.

• Agility

Participants: 2 goalkeepers	**Equipment:**	2 balls
Coach		2 marker flags

Key aspects
- Endurance
- Agility
- Diving to stop high to medium-high shots
- Take-off strength
- Catching the ball securely

Variations
- Diving to stop low shots
- Reaction speed

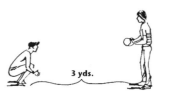

3 yds.

Starting position
The goalkeeper squats facing the coach, who stands 3 yards away holding a ball.

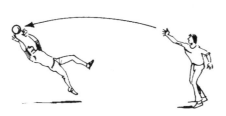

Phase 1
The coach throws the ball in an arc over the goalkeeper's head. The goalkeeper leaps backward and catches the ball.

Phase 2
Immediately after landing, the goalkeeper throws the ball back to the coach.

Phase 3
The coach catches the ball and the goalkeeper resumes his squatting position. The coach then throws the high to medium-high to the goalkeeper's left.

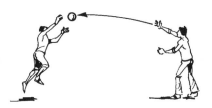

Phase 4
The goalkeeper dives to his left and catches the ball, which he then throws back to the coach.

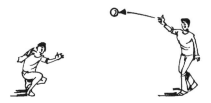

Phase 5
The coach catches the ball and the goalkeeper resumes his squatting position. The coach then throws the ball high to medium-high to the goalkeeper's right, and so on.

Variations
The coach throws the ball low or high to medium-high to either side of the goalkeeper at random.

• **Endurance**

Participants: 1 goalkeeper Coach	**Equipment:** 1 ball

Starting position
The goalkeeper squats facing the coach, who stands 3 yards away holding a ball.

3 yds.

Phase 1
The coach lobs the ball high to the goalkeeper. The goalkeeper leaps forward toward the ball.

Phase 2
The goalkeeper catches the ball and immediately throws the ball back to the coach.

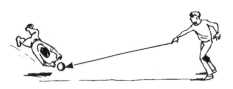

Phase 3
The coach now throws the ball low to the goalkeeper's right. The goalkeeper dives to catch the ball.

• Endurance

95

Phase 4
While still on the ground, the goalkeeper throws the ball back to the coach.

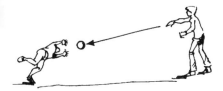

Phase 5
Phases 1 and 2 are repeated, then the coach throws the ball low to the goalkeeper's left, and so on.

Variations
After throwing a high ball, the coach throws the ball to either side of the goalkeeper at random.

• Endurance

Participants: 1 goalkeeper
Coach

Equipment: 1 ball

3 yds.

Starting position
The goalkeeper lies on his back with feet pointing toward the coach, who stands 3 yards away. The goalkeeper's arms are stretched straight out behind his head.

Phase 1
The coach throws the ball so that it falls toward the goalkeeper's waist. The goalkeeper sits up and catches the ball.

Phase 2
The goalkeeper throws the ball back to the coach, who throws it above the goalkeeper's head. The goalkeeper springs to his feet and jumps into the air to catch the ball.

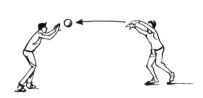

Phase 3
The goalkeeper throws the ball back to the coach and then quickly lies face down with his head toward the coach.

• Endurance

Phase 4
The coach throws a medium-high ball to the goalkeeper, who raises his upper body from the ground and catches the ball in front of his head.

Phase 5
The goalkeeper throws the ball back to the coach and lies face down again. The coach then throws the ball high to the goalkeeper.

Phase 6
The goalkeeper springs to his feet and jumps into the air to catch the ball. He throws the ball back to the coach, then quickly lies on his back again, and so on

• Endurance

Participants: 1 goalkeeper	Equipment: 1 ball
Coach	

Starting position

Eight balls are distributed over the ground with gaps of 3 to 4 yards between them. Depending on the distance the goalkeeper can dive, this distance can be increased. The coach and the goalkeeper stand about 3 yards away from the balls.

Phase 1

At a call from the coach the goalkeeper dives to one of the balls and clasps it securely in both hands.

Phase 2

As quickly as possible the goalkeeper puts the ball back in its place, springs to his feet and dives toward he next ball, and so on.

• **Endurance**

99

Variations
1. The coach calls "left", "right" or "straight ahead" to indicate which ball the goalkeeper should dive at.

2. After replacing the ball the goalkeeper turns through 360 degrees and dives to the next one.

3. The goalkeeper stands with his back to the next ball. He then makes a half-turn and dives in one fluid movement.

4. While the goalkeeper is still on the ground, the coach kneels on all fours to form an obstacle over which the goalkeeper must dive to grasp the next ball. The coach constantly changes the direction in which the goalkeeper has to dive.

5. The balls are arranged in a zigzag pattern.

6. The balls are arranged in a line.

4.

Participants: 1 goalkeeper
Coach

Equipment: 8 balls

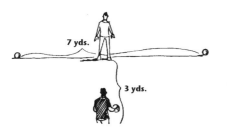

Starting position
The goalkeeper stands in the middle of a goal formed by 2 balls placed 7 yards apart. He faces the coach, who stands 3 yards away holding a ball.

Phase 1
The coach throws the ball high to the goalkeeper, who jumps to meet it and catches it as high as possible.

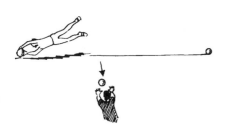

Phase 2
The goalkeeper throws the ball back to coach and immediately dives to the ball on his right and clasps it to his body.

• Endurance

Phase 3
The goalkeeper replaces the ball, runs round it, turns toward the coach and performs a forward roll over the ball.

Phase 4
As he comes out of his forward roll the goalkeeper sprints back to the middle of the goal and jumps to catch the next high ball thrown by the coach. The goalkeeper throws the ball back to the coach then dives to the ball on his left and clasps it to his body, and so on.

Variation
The coach uses a medicine ball for the high throw to the goalkeeper.

• Endurance

Participants:	1 goalkeeper	Equipment:	3 balls
	Coach	Variation:	2 balls
			1 medicine ball

Key aspects
- Endurance
- Agility
- Diving to stop low shots
- Diving to stop high to medium-high shots

- Rolling away to the side
- Take-off strength
- Catching the ball securely
- Deflecting the ball
- Punching the ball
- Speed off the mark

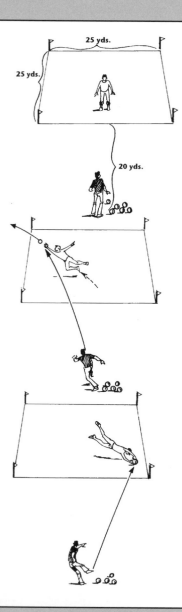

25 yds.

25 yds.

20 yds.

Starting position

A square measuring 25 x 25 yards is formed by placing marker flags at each corner. The goalkeeper stands in the middle of this square. He faces the coach, who stands 20 yards outside the square. The coach has a ball at his feet and another 5 balls are on the ground nearby.

Phase 1

The coach plays the ball low, high or medium-high into the square. The goalkeeper has the task of running to the ball and gathering it, or jumping or diving to catch, punch or deflect the ball. The ball must not touch the ground inside the square.

Phase 2

As soon as the goalkeeper has dealt with the first ball the coach plays the second one into the square. He varies the speed and direction of the ball, so that the goalkeeper is continuously on the move. The coach puts the goalkeeper under pressure but must always give him a chance of reaching the ball. If the goalkeeper catches the ball he throws it back to the coach.

Participants: 1 goalkeeper
Coach

Equipment: 1 ball

• **Endurance**

Key aspects	• Reaction speed
• Endurance	• Catching the ball securely
• Agility	**Variations 1 and 2**
• Diving to stop low shots	• Diving to stop high to medium-
• Take-off strength	high shots

Starting position
The goalkeeper stands on the 18-yard line, holding a ball. He faces the coach, who stands 5 yards away.

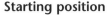
5 yds.

Phase 1
The goalkeeper throws the ball waist-high to the coach, who plays it back low to the goalkeeper's right or left.

Phase 2
The goalkeeper dives to catch the ball and immediately springs to his feet. The coach changes position to face the goalkeeper directly again. The coach can play the ball to right or left of the goalkeeper at random, so the two continuously move back and forth along the 18-yard line.

Variations
1. The coach plays the ball back high to medium-high.
2. The coach varies the speed and height of the ball and the side to which he kicks it.

• Endurance

| **Participants:** 1 goalkeeper | **Equipment:** 1 ball |
| Coach | 1 penalty area |

Key aspects

- Endurance
- Agility
- Diving to stop low shots
- Diving to stop high to medium-high shots
- Catching the ball when diving forward

- Take-off strength
- Catching the ball securely
- Speed off the mark

Variations 1 and 2

- Reaction speed
- Punching the ball with one fist
- Deflecting the ball

Starting position

The goalkeeper stands in the middle of the goal. A ball lies on the goal line 1 or 2 yards inside his right-hand post. The coach stands facing him on the penalty spot, holding a ball. Another 7 balls lie on the ground nearby.

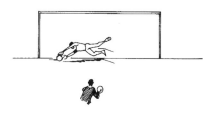

Phase 1

At a call from the coach the goalkeeper dives to grasp the ball on the goal line. He clasps the ball to his body with both hands.

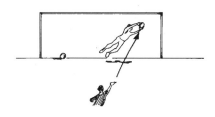

Phase 2

The goalkeeper replaces the ball and turns to face the coach. The coach throws the ball high to medium-high toward the goalkeeper's left. The goalkeeper dives to catch the ball with both hands.

• Endurance

Phase 3
While still on the ground the goalkeeper rolls the ball back to the coach. In the meantime the coach has picked up the next ball. He lobs it steeply into the air so that it falls between the goal line and the penalty spot.

Phase 4
The goalkeeper springs to his feet and sprints forward and dives to catch the ball before it bounces or just as it reaches the ground. The goalkeeper rolls the ball back to the coach and resumes his starting position on the goal line, and so on.

Variations
1. The coach throws the ball high to half-high toward the corner of the goal, so that the goalkeeper can only deflect it wide of the goal.

2. After gathering the ball and rolling it back to the coach as described in phase 4, the goalkeeper backpedals toward the goal line as fast as possible. At the same time the coach lobs up the next ball so that it falls toward the crossbar. As he moves back, the goalkeeper leaps backward and deflects or punches the ball over the bar.

• **Endurance**

Participants: 1 goalkeeper	Equipment:	8 balls
Coach		1 goal
		1 penalty area

Key aspects
- Endurance
- Agility
- Diving to stop low shots
- Speed off the mark
- Throwing the ball into play

Variations 1 and 2
- Kicking the ball into play

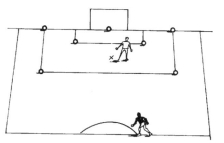

Starting position
The goalkeeper stands on the penalty spot. A ball lies in the middle of the goal line, at each infield corner of the goal area and at each corner of the penalty area. The coach stands near the midfield line.

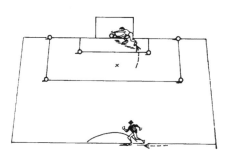

Phase 1
At a call from the coach the goalkeeper sprints to the goal, dives on the ball on the goal line and clasps it to his body with both hands.

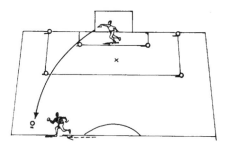

Phase 2
The goalkeeper springs to his feet and throws the ball overarm, with either a straight or bent arm, into the path of the coach, who is running along the center line. The coach picks up the ball and places it on the center line.

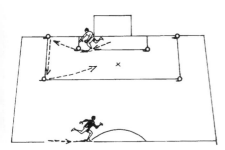

Phase 3
The goalkeeper sprints to the ball at the right corner of the goal area, then to the balls at each corner on the right of the penalty area, etc. In each case the coach runs along the center line to receive the goalkeeper's throw.

Variations
1. The goalkeeper drops the ball and volleys or half-volleys it instead of throwing it.
2. The coach stands 15 yards beyond the center line in the other half of the pitch.

Endurance

Participant:	1 goalkeeper	Equipment:	7 balls
	Coach		1 goal
			1 half of the pitch
		Variation 2:	1 full pitch

Key aspects	
• Endurance	• Rolling away to the side
• Agility	• Take-off strength
• Diving to stop low shots	• Reaction speed
• Diving to stop high to medium-high shots	• Catching the ball securely
	• Punching the ball
• Deflecting the ball	• Speed off the mark

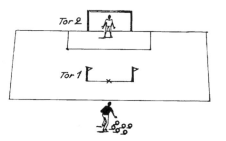

Starting position

The goalkeeper stands on the goal line of goal 2. The coach stands just outside the penalty area with 6 balls nearby. A marker flag is positioned on each side of the penalty spot to form another goal (goal 1).

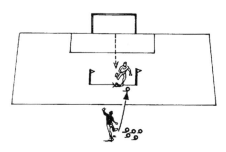

Phase 1

The coach plays the ball along the ground toward goal 1. The goalkeeper sprints from goal 2 to goal 1 and tries to gather the ball before it crosses the goal line.

Endurance

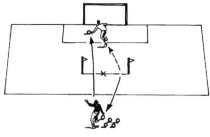

Phase 2

The goalkeeper rolls the ball to the coach and runs back toward goal 2. At the same time the coach shoots low, high or medium-high at goal 2. The goalkeeper must always have a chance of stopping the ball before it crosses the line.

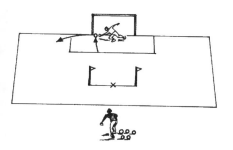

Phase 3

As he runs back, the goalkeeper tries to catch, punch or deflect the second ball before it can cross the goal line of goal 2. If he catches the ball he rolls it back to the coach. He resumes his starting position, and so on.

Variations

1. The coach plays the ball low, high or medium-high toward goal 1.

2. The coach lobs the ball toward goal 1 so that the goalkeeper has to jump to catch the ball.

3. The coach lobs the ball toward goal 2 so that the goalkeeper has to jump and deflect or punch the ball wide of the goal as he runs back.

• **Endurance**

Participants: 1 goalkeeper	**Equipment:** 6 balls
Coach	1 goal
	1 penalty area
	2 marker flags

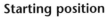

Key aspects	
• Endurance	• Take-off strength
• Agility	• Catching the ball securely
• Diving to stop high to medium-high shots	• Lower leg flexors
	• Back of the leg muscles
	• Trunk muscles

3 yds.

3 yds.

Starting position

The goalkeeper sits on the line marking the edge of the penalty area with his legs stretched out straight and slightly apart. He faces the coach, who stands 3 yards away from him at the point where the line marking the edge of the penalty area meets the goal line.

Phase 1

The coach throws the ball over the goalkeeper so that it falls behind him and to the side. The goalkeeper pushes himself up and dives to catch the ball.

Phase 2

On landing, the goalkeeper throws the ball back to the coach. He then sits again. The coach moves so that he is still facing the goalkeeper directly. He catches the ball and as soon as the goalkeeper is sitting he throws it over his head again. The two of them repeat this until they reach the 18-yard line.

Phase 3

The goalkeeper now recuperates actively by performing a gymnastic exercise. He stands upright with his legs together and bends forward, keeping his legs straight, trying to touch the ground with his palms. He stands upright and repeats this a few times. Meanwhile the coach takes up a position 3 yards away from the goalkeeper on the 18-yard line.

• Endurance

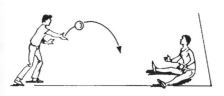

Phase 4

At a call from the coach the goalkeeper stops the gymnastic exercise and sits on the ground facing the coach. The coach throws the ball high to medium-high so that it falls in front of the goalkeeper.

Phase 5

The goalkeeper dives forward to catch the ball. He throws it back to the coach, who takes a few paces back to maintain the distance of 3 yards between them. The coach catches the ball, and so on.

Phase 6

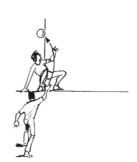

When the other side of the penalty area is reached the goalkeeper stands with legs apart, clasps his hands behind his head and bends to right and left alternately, bouncing 3 times on each side. The upper body must not bend forward but only to the side. Meanwhile the coach takes up a position 3 yards away from the goalkeeper on the final line marking the edge of the penalty area.

Phase 7

The coach again throws the ball so that it falls behind the goalkeeper (as described in phases 1 and 2).

Variations

1. On the two parallel sides of the penalty area the coach throws the ball so that it falls in front of the goalkeeper and on the 18-yard line he throws it so that it falls behind the goalkeeper.

2. The coach and the goalkeeper follow a path across the pitch from sideline to sideline. On the first leg the coach throws the ball so that it falls behind the goalkeeper. At the end of the first leg the goalkeeper recuperates by carrying out a gymnastic exercise (as described in phase 3 or 6). On the return leg the coach throws the ball so that it falls in front of the goalkeeper.

• Endurance

Participants: 1 goalkeeper	Equipment:	1 ball
Coach		Penalty area
	Variation 2:	1 half of the pitch

Key aspects
- Endurance
- Agility
- Diving to stop low shots
- Diving to stop high to medium-high shots
- Take-off strength
- Reaction speed
- Catching the ball securely

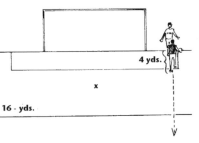

Starting position

The goalkeeper stands on the goal line to the left of the goal. He faces the coach, who is 4 yards away and is holding a ball. Each of them has the task of getting to the center line as fast as possible.

Phase 1

The coach throws the ball in random sequence either low or high or medium-high to the goalkeeper's right or left or directly at his body. The goalkeeper dives forward to catch the ball, thus moving closer to the center line.

Phase 2

The goalkeeper catches the ball securely in both hands and throws it back to the coach, who has moved back toward the center line to maintain his distance from the goalkeeper. The coach catches the ball and throws it to the goalkeeper, who springs to his feet and dives forward to catch the ball again, and so on.

• Endurance

Participants: 1 goalkeeper	Equipment: 1 ball
Coach	1 half pitch

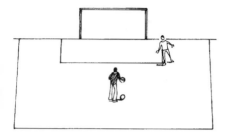

Starting position

The goalkeeper stands in front and to the left of his goal, at the end of the 6-yard line. The coach is standing on the penalty spot holding a ball. Another ball lies to his right.

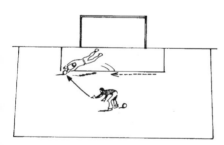

Phase 1

At a call from the coach the goalkeeper sprints to the other end of the 6-yard line. The coach rolls the ball toward this corner of the goal area at a speed that will allow the goalkeeper to reach it. While running the goalkeeper dives onto the ball and clasps it securely to his body with both hands.

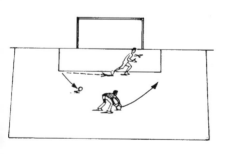

Phase 2

While still on the ground the goalkeeper throws the ball back to the coach, springs to his feet and sprints back to the other end of the 6-yard line. At the same time the coach takes the second ball and rolls it toward the corner of the goal area so that he can dive on it, and so on.

Variations

1. The coach throws the ball high to medium-high.
2. The coach stands in the middle of the 6-yard line with his back to the goal, while the goalkeeper sprints along the 18-yard line.

• Endurance

Participants: 1 goalkeeper
Coach

Equipment: 2 balls
penalty area

114

Key aspects
- Take-off strength
  (running take-off from one foot)
- Speed off the mark

Variation
Reaction speed

Starting position
The goalkeeper stands 1 yard in front of the middle of the goal with his back to the goal.

Phase 1
The goalkeeper sprints to his right, takes off from one foot and touches the angle of the post and crossbar.

Phase 2
On landing, the goalkeeper turns round and sprints toward the other goalpost.

Phase 3
The goalkeeper takes off from one foot and touches the angle of post and crossbar, and so on.

Variations
The coach calls out as the goalkeeper is running along the goal line and the goalkeeper jumps up and touches the crossbar.

Take-off strength

Participant:	1 goalkeeper	Equipment:	1 goal
Variation:	Coach		

Starting position
The goalkeeper squats 1 yard in front of the middle of the goal with his back to the goal.

1 yd.

Phase 1
The goalkeeper leaps up powerfully. While in the air he turns 45 degrees to his left (or right) and swings both arms up above his head. As he comes out of the turn he touches the crossbar with his left (or right) hand while holding the other arm downward for balance. His eyes are fixed on the point on the crossbar where his hand makes contact.

Phase 2
The goalkeeper lands on both feet and sinks down into a squatting position again. Still squatting, he jumps and turns to resume his starting position, then uses his momentum for his next leap to touch the crossbar, and so on.

Variations
The goalkeeper turns clockwise and counter-clockwise alternately.

• Take-off strength

Participant: 1 goalkeeper   **Equipment:** 1 goal

Starting position
The goalkeeper squats facing one of the goal posts at a distance of 2 feet.

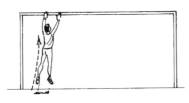

Phase 1
The goalkeeper leaps up, stretches both arms above his head and touches the crossbar with the palms of both hands.

Phase 2
The goalkeeper lands on both feet and sinks down into a squatting position again. Still squatting, he jumps 1 to 2 feet toward the other goal post, leaps up again, and so on.

• Take-off strength

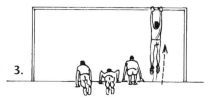

Variations

1. The goalkeeper holds a medicine ball. He leaps up and touches the crossbar with the medicine ball.

2. The goalkeeper sits on the goal line with his knees bent, supporting himself with his arms to the side. From this position he pushes himself powerfully to his feet, leaps upward and touches the crossbar with one hand. He then sits on the goal line again, and so on.

3. The goalkeeper lies 2 feet in front of the goal in the press-up position with his head pointing toward the goal. He performs a push-up, draws his legs forward so that he is in the squatting position, and leaps up to touch the crossbar. He lands in the squatting position and immediately assumes the push-up position again.

4. The goalkeeper stands 2 feet in front of the goal. He jumps as high as he can from the standing position, swinging his arms to achieve greater momentum. The aim is to jump so high that his head is level with the crossbar. While in the air he pushes his hips forward and pulls his upper body and legs backward.

• Take-off strength

Participant: 1 goalkeeper	Equipment: 1 goal
	Variation 1: 1 medicine ball

Starting position
2 balls lie on the 6-yard line directly in front of the goal. The goalkeeper stands behind the balls, facing the goal.

Phase 1
The goalkeeper picks up the ball on his left and runs toward the goal post on his left.

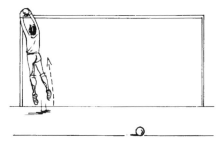

Phase 2
Just before he reaches the goal post he stops, braces himself with his legs apart, jumps up, taking off from both feet, and presses the ball with both hands against the angle of the goalpost and crossbar.

• Take-off strength

Phase 3

After landing, he immediately sprints back to the 6-yard line, picks up the other ball, sprints to the goalpost on his right, and so on

Variations

1. 2 medicine balls lie on the 6-yard line.
2. Before the goalkeeper jumps, he sinks into the squatting position.

• Take-off strength

Participant:	1 goalkeeper	Equipment:	2 balls
			1 goal
			1 goal area
		Variation 1:	2 medicine balls

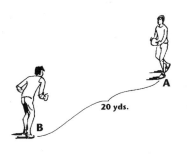

Starting position
The goalkeepers face each other at a distance of 20 yards. Goalkeeper A holds the ball.

Phase 1
Goalkeeper A lets the ball fall and volleys it with his instep to goalkeeper B.

Phase 2
Goalkeeper A falls face down on the ground with his legs and arms stretched out straight, while goalkeeper B jumps to catch the ball as high as possible.

• **Take-off strength**

Phase 3

After catching the ball, goalkeeper B clasps it securely to his chest, then rolls it to goalkeeper A, who has sprung to his feet again. Goalkeeper A gathers the ball, and so on. After 5 cycles the goalkeepers swap roles.

Variations

1. The ball is rolled back slightly to the side of goalkeeper A, so that he has to move or kneel to the side to gather it.

2. Goalkeeper A throws the ball at goalkeeper B's body so that it bounces up at him. Goalkeeper B dives forward and punches the ball away.

• **Take-off strength**

Participants: 2 goalkeepers   **Equipment:** 1 ball

Starting position

The goalkeepers stand side by side, 2 yards apart. The coach stands facing them at a distance of 3 yards and is holding a ball.

Phase 1

The goalkeeper lobs the ball up toward the 2 goalkeepers. The goalkeepers both jump up and try to catch the ball.

Phase 2

The aim is to catch the ball in both hands. If the ball is deflected but not caught, both goalkeepers go after the loose ball and try to gather it. The ball is then played back to the coach and the goalkeepers resume their positions, and so on.

• Take-off strength

123

Variations

1. The goalkeepers stand with their backs to the coach, who calls out when he throws the ball.

2. The coach stands 5 yards away from the goalkeepers. He throws the ball up high in front of his body and then moves aside. The goalkeepers sprint toward the ball and jump to catch it.

3. The coach stands 8 to 10 yards away from the goalkeepers. As soon as the coach throws the ball up high in front of his body and moves aside, the goalkeepers perform a forward roll and sprint toward the ball to try and catch it before it touches the ground.

4. The goalkeepers sit back-to-back on the ground, with their legs stretched out straight and slightly apart. They watch the coach, who stands 3 yards away from them. As soon as the coach throws the ball up high in front of his body they jump up and sprint to catch it.

5. The goalkeepers lie face down 3 yards apart, with arms straight out ahead of them on the ground, extending toward the coach, who stands 3 yards away from them and throws the ball up high so that it falls between the goalkeepers.

6. The goalkeepers lie on their backs with their legs pointing toward the coach.

7. The coach awards points. The goalkeeper who wins the ball scores one point.

2.

5 yds.

3.

8-10 yds.

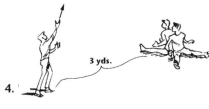

4.

3 yds.

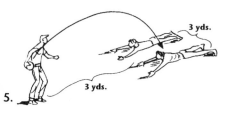

5.

3 yds.

3 yds.

• Take-off strength

Participants: 2 goalkeepers
Coach

Equipment: 1 ball

124

Key aspects
- Take-off strength
- Agility
- Catching the ball securely
- Leg extensors
- Lower arm extensors
- Shoulder muscles

Variations
- Abdominal muscles
- Hip flexors

Starting position
Goalkeeper A, who is holding a ball, stands 2 yards in front of goalkeeper B, who performs a push-up.

Phase 1
Goalkeeper A lobs the ball up high in front of his body and falls into the push-up position. Goalkeeper B springs to his feet and jumps to catch the ball.

Phase 2
Goalkeeper A performs a push-up as goalkeeper B catches the ball at the highest possible point of its path. When goalkeeper B lands, he throws the ball up high again, and so on.

Variations
Before goalkeeper A throws the ball up, goalkeeper B, who is lying on his back, raises his legs and upper body and touches his toes (jack-knife).

Participants: 2 goalkeepers   **Equipment:** 1 ball

• Take-off strength

125

Starting position
The goalkeeper stands in the middle of the goal, facing the coach, who is standing on the penalty spot holding a ball.

Phase 1
The coach lobs the ball high into the air so that it falls near the goal. The goalkeeper runs toward the ball and makes a running take-off from one foot to catch the ball.

Phase 2
The goalkeeper catches the ball at the highest possible point of its path. As he lands he sinks into the squatting position, throws the ball back to the coach and sprints back to his starting position. The coach throws the ball up again, and so on.

Variations
The coach stands 8 yards to the right or left of the penalty spot. The goalkeeper runs to the corresponding side and takes-off from one foot.

• Take-off strength

Participants:	1 goalkeeper	Equipment:	1 ball
	Coach		1 goal
			1 goal area

Starting position
The goalkeeper squats on the goal line, facing the coach, who is standing 6 yards away holding a ball.

Phase 1
The coach lobs the ball up high toward the crossbar. The goalkeeper jumps and catches the ball at crossbar height.

Phase 2
The goalkeeper clasps the ball securely to his chest, then throws it back to the coach and sinks into the squatting position again. As soon as the goalkeeper is in position the coach lobs the ball up high again, and so on.

• **Take-off strength**

127

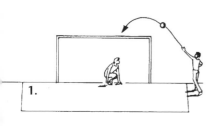

Variations

1. The coach stands to the side of the goal, just outside the goal area, and lobs the ball up so that it falls toward the crossbar.

2. The goalkeeper lies in the push-up position. At a call from the coach he squats, jumps up and catches the ball thrown by the coach at the height of the crossbar. He throws the ball back to the coach, sinks into the squatting position and then returns to the push-up position.

3. The coach has 6 balls available. He throws the balls up high toward the crossbar in such a way that the goalkeeper can only punch or deflect the ball over the crossbar with one hand.

4. The coach throws a medicine ball.

• Take-off strength

Participants:	1 goalkeeper	Equipment:	1 ball
	Coach		1 goal
		Variation 1:	1 goal area
		Variation 3:	6 balls
		Variation 4:	1 medicine ball

- Take-off strength
- Agility
- Diving to stop low shots
- Reaction speed

Variation
- Catching the ball securely
- Leg extensors

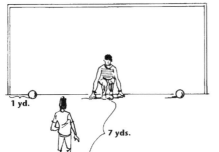

Starting position
The goalkeeper squats in the middle of the goal, facing the coach, who is standing 7 yards away. A ball lies in each half of the goal, 1 foot from the goal line and 1 yard from the goalpost.

Phase 1
The coach calls out "right" or "left" and the goalkeeper dives explosively to the corresponding ball to his right or left and clasps it with both hands.

Phase 2
The goalkeeper replaces the ball and resumes his starting position as quickly as possible. The coach calls again and the goalkeeper again dives to the appropriate ball. The direction sequence is random.

Variation
The coach holds another ball. He throws it up high toward the goalkeeper, who jumps up from the squatting position and catches it at crossbar height. The goalkeeper sinks into the squatting position again and throws the ball back to then coach. The coach then calls out "right" or "left" and the goalkeeper dives to the corresponding ball as described in phase 1.

• Take-off strength

Participants:	1 goalkeeper	Equipment:	2 balls
	Coach		1 goal
		Variation:	3 balls

Starting position

The goalkeeper stands with his legs slightly apart. His arms are stretched out to the side, parallel to the ground, and he is holding a ball in his right hand. His eyes are directed toward the ball.

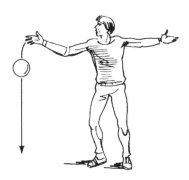

Phase 1

The goalkeeper lets the ball fall to the ground.

Phase 2

The goalkeeper tries to catch the ball with both hands before it touches the ground, and so on.

• Reaction speed

Participant: 1 goalkeeper   **Equipment:** 1 ball

Variation 2
- Diving to stop low shots
- Diving to stop high to medium-high shots

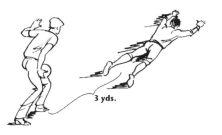

Starting position
The goalkeeper lies face down with his arms extended forward and his legs pointing toward the coach, who is holding a ball.

Phase 1
The coach calls out and rolls the ball to the right or left of the goalkeeper. As an aid, he can initially call out "right" or "left" to indicate where the ball is.

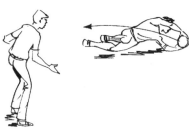

Phase 2
The goalkeeper turns quickly toward the ball and has to gather it with both hands. He throws the ball back to the coach and lies face down again, and so on.

Variations
1. The goalkeeper lies on his back instead of face down.
2. The coach calls out and throws the ball low, high or medium-high to the left or right of the goalkeeper, who is lying face down or on his back. The goalkeeper has to dive and catch the ball.

Reaction speed

Participants: 1 goalkeeper
Coach

Equipment: 1 ball

Starting position
The goalkeeper kneels facing the coach, who stands 3 yards away holding a ball. The goalkeeper's arms hang down at his sides.

3 yds.

Phase 1
The coach throws the ball above head height. It can be directed at random over the goalkeeper's head or over his right or left shoulder.

Phase 2
The goalkeeper raises both arms quickly above his head and punches the ball back to the coach with both fists. The coach catches the ball and throws it again as soon as the goalkeeper's arms are hanging at his side again.

• Reaction speed

Participants: 1 goalkeeper
Coach

Equipment: 1 ball

Key aspects
- Reaction speed
- Agility
- Diving to stop low shots
- Diving to stop high to medium-high shots

- Take-off strength
- Catching the ball securely
- Deflecting the ball

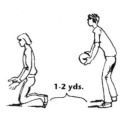

1-2 yds.

Starting position
The goalkeeper kneels with his back to the coach, who stands 1 or 2 yards away holding a ball.

Phase 1
The coach calls out and throws the ball high over the goalkeeper's head so that it falls in front of him.

Phase 2
As soon as the coach calls out, the goalkeeper tries to gauge the path of the ball so that he can catch it or deflect it before it touches the ground. If the goalkeeper only deflects the ball or cannot reach it before it touches the ground, he must dive after it and gather it securely. The goalkeeper throws the ball back to the coach and resumes his starting position.

• Reaction speed

133

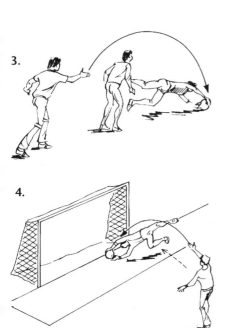

3.

4.

Variations

1. The coach throws the ball so that it lands to the right or left of the goalkeeper.

2. The coach throws the ball without first calling out.

3. The coach stands instead of kneeling. The coach throws the ball high over the goalkeeper's head so that it comes down to the goalkeeper's right or left and the goalkeeper has to cover more ground to reach the ball. The goalkeeper dives to catch the ball.

4. The goalkeeper stands outside the goal area, facing the center of the goal. The coach stands behind him. The coach throws the ball over the goalkeeper's head, possibly calling out at the same time, and the goalkeeper has to stop the ball from crossing the goal line.

● **Reaction speed**

Participants: 1 goalkeeper	**Equipment:** 1 ball
Coach	**Variation 4:** 1 goal
	1 goal area

Key aspects
- Reaction speed
- Agility
- Diving to stop low shots
- Diving to stop high to medium-high shots
- Take-off strength
- Catching the ball securely

Starting position
The goalkeeper stands with his back to the coach, who stands 5 yards away holding a ball.

5 yds.

Phase 1
The coach calls out and throws the ball low or high to medium-high alternately to the right and left of the goalkeeper. As an aid the coach can call out the side to which he will throw.

Phase 2
As soon as the coach calls out, the goalkeeper turns and dives to catch the ball securely. The goalkeeper must turn through the longest possible path before diving for the ball. If the coach throws to his right, the goalkeeper has to turn counter-clockwise, and if the ball is thrown to his left he has to turn clockwise. After catching the ball the goalkeeper throws it back to the coach and resumes his starting position.

Participants: 1 goalkeeper
Coach

Equipment: 1 ball

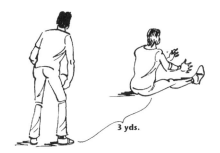

Starting position
The goalkeeper sits with his back to the coach, who stands 3 yards away holding a ball.

Phase 1
The coach lifts the ball above his head and throws it hard onto the ground, so that it bounces over the goalkeeper and falls again in front of him.

Phase 2
The goalkeeper springs to his feet as soon as he hears the ball hit the ground. He dives forward to catch it before it touches the ground. He then throws the ball back to the coach and resumes his starting position, and so on.

Variations
The coach bounces the ball so that it falls to the left or right in front of the goalkeeper.

• Reaction speed

Participants: 1 goalkeeper
Coach

Equipment: 1 ball

Key aspects
- Reaction speed
- Agility
- Diving to stop high to medium-high shots
- Take-off strength
- Catching the ball securely

Starting position

The goalkeeper stands with his back to the coach, who stands 5 yards away holding a ball.

5 yds.

Phase 1

The coach lifts the ball above his head and throws it hard onto the ground, so that it bounces high to medium-high toward the goalkeeper. The coach constantly changes the side to which he throws.

Phase 2

The goalkeeper turns as soon as he hears the ball hit the ground. He dives and tries to catch it before it touches the ground. He then throws the ball back to the coach and resumes his starting position, and so on.

Variations

Instead of standing, the goalkeeper squats, sits with his legs apart, kneels or lies face down.

• Reaction speed

Participants: 1 goalkeeper
Coach

Equipment: 1 ball

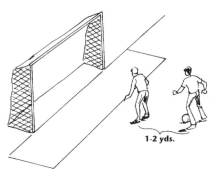

Starting position
The goalkeeper stands just outside the goal area, facing the center of the goal, with his back to the coach, who stands 1 or 2 yards away with a ball at his feet.

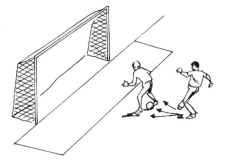

Phase 1
The coach calls to the goalkeeper and sidefoots the ball between the goalkeeper's legs. The coach randomly changes the direction in which he kicks the ball (straight, to the left, or to the right).

Phase 2
The goalkeeper must prevent the ball from crossing the goal line. He dives to catch or deflect the ball and then clasps it securely to his chest. He then throws the ball back to the coach and resumes his starting position, and so on.

Variations
1. The coach gradually kicks the ball harder.
2. The coach plays the ball without calling out to the goalkeeper.

• **Reaction speed**

Participants: 1 goalkeeper	**Equipment:** 1 ball
Coach	1 goal
	1 goal area

Starting position

The goalkeeper stands with his back to the coach, who stands 2 yards away holding a ball.

Phase 1

The coach lobs the ball over the goalkeeper's head so that it falls 3 to 5 yards in front of him.

Phase 2

As soon as the goalkeeper can gauge the path of the ball he sprints after it. He has to dive and catch it before it touches the ground or at least after the first bounce. He then throws the ball back to the coach and resumes his starting position, and so on.

Variations

The goalkeeper faces the coach. As soon as the coach throws the ball the goalkeeper spins round and tries to reach it.

• Reaction speed

Participants:	1 goalkeeper	Equipment:	1 ball
	Coach		

Starting position

The goalkeeper stands just outside the goal area with his legs apart. He has his back to the center of the goal and is facing the coach, who stands 1 or 2 yards away with a ball at his feet.

Phase 1

The coach sidefoots the ball between the goalkeeper's legs. The coach randomly changes the direction in which he kicks the ball (straight, to the left, or to the right).

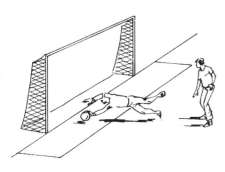

Phase 2

The goalkeeper turns alternately to right and left and dives to catch the ball. He must prevent the ball from crossing the goal line. He catches or deflects the ball and then clasps it securely to his chest. He then throws the ball back to the coach and resumes his starting position, and so on.

Variation

The coach kicks the ball harder.

• Reaction speed

Participants: 1 goalkeeper Coach	**Equipment:** 1 ball 1 goal 1 goal area

Key aspects
- Reaction speed
- Agility
- Diving to stop low shots

- Diving to stop high to medium-high shots
- Take-off strength
- Catching the ball securely

Starting position
The goalkeeper stands on the 6-yard line level in line with his left-hand post. He faces along the 6-yard line across the face of the goal and has his back to the coach, who is standing at the end of the 6-yard line holding a ball.

Phase 1
The goalkeeper runs forward along the 6-yard line. The coach calls out and throws the ball low, high or medium-high behind the goalkeeper's back toward the goal.

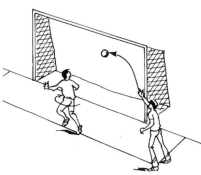

Phase 2
The goalkeeper turns to the right and dives to catch the ball. He then throws the ball back to the coach and resumes his starting position, and so on.

• Reaction speed

Participants:	1 goalkeeper	Equipment:	1 ball
	Coach		1 goal
			1 goal area

Key aspects
- Reaction speed
- Agility
- Catching the ball securely
- Deflecting the ball

Starting position
The goalkeeper squats facing the coach, who stands 1 yard away. The coach's arms are held straight out to the side and he is holding a ball in each hand.

Phase 1
The coach allows a ball to fall from one hand.

Phase 2
The goalkeeper dives to catch the ball before it touches the ground, or to deflect it and then clasp it to his chest. If he cannot prevent the ball from touching the ground he should try to block it on the first bounce. When he has secured the ball he throws it back to the coach and resumes his starting position, and so on.

• Reaction speed

Participants: 1 goalkeeper
Coach

Equipment: 2 balls

Key aspects	
• Reaction speed	• Catching the ball securely
• Agility	• Deflecting the ball

Starting position

The goalkeeper stands with his back to the coach, who stands 3 yards away holding a ball in each hand.

Phase 1

The coach calls out and lobs the 2 balls simultaneously to the goalkeeper. The paths of the balls must not be too far apart.

Phase 2

The goalkeeper turns quickly and tries to catch the 2 balls and clasp them to his chest. If he cannot catch them he must try to deflect them to the side and then to grab one of them. He throws the balls back to the coach and resumes his starting position, and so on.

• Reaction speed

Participants: 1 goalkeeper Coach	**Equipment:** 2 balls

Starting position
The goalkeeper lies in the push-up position with his legs pointing toward the coach, who stands 3 yards away holding a ball. Another 5 balls lie on the ground nearby.

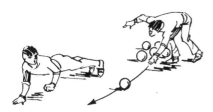

Phase 1
The coach calls out and rolls a ball at random to the right or left of the goalkeeper.

Phase 2
The goalkeeper throws himself to the side to deflect the ball. The coach picks up the next ball and the coach returns to his starting position, and so on.

Variations
1. The coach throws the ball high to medium-high instead of rolling it.
2. The goalkeeper lies in the push-up position, but with his head toward the coach.

• Reaction speed

Participants: 1 goalkeeper
Coach

Equipment: 6 balls

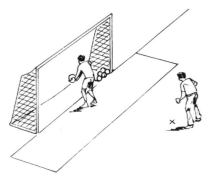

Starting position

The goalkeeper stands in the middle of the goal with his back to the coach, who is standing near the penalty spot. The goalkeeper is holding a ball. Another 5 balls lie on the ground in the goal.

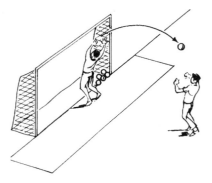

Phase 1

The goalkeeper throws the ball 2-handed back over his head in a high arc to the coach and turns to face the coach. He turns alternately clockwise and counter-clockwise.

• **Reaction speed**

Phase 2
The coach heads the ball at goal. (He can head it while stationary or running, with his feet on the ground or in the air.) He tries to score, while still giving the goalkeeper a chance to stop the ball. The goalkeeper can catch, punch or deflect the ball. He takes the same ball or picks up one of the other balls in the goal and resumes his starting position, and so on.

Variations
1. The goalkeeper assumes a squatting rather than a standing starting position.
2. The coach stands closer to the goal (5 to 7 yards).
3. The coach stands on the penalty spot and volleys or side-volleys the ball powerfully at goal instead of heading it. He tries to shoot at, or within 3 or 4 feet of, the goalkeeper's body, so that the goalkeeper has a chance of stopping the shot.

• Reaction speed

Participants: 1 goalkeeper	**Equipment:** 6 balls
Coach	1 goal
	1 penalty area

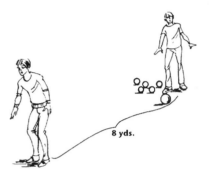

Starting position

The goalkeeper stands with his back to the coach, who stands 8 yards behind him. Six balls lie on the ground beside the coach.

8 yds.

Phase 1

The coach calls out and shoots close enough to the goalkeeper to give him a chance of reaching the shot. The coach constantly varies the height and direction of the shot. When the goalkeeper hears the coach's call he turns, sizes up the situation and reacts accordingly by diving or jumping to catch, punch or deflect the ball.

Phase 2

If the goalkeeper catches the ball he throws it back to the coach, otherwise the coach takes a ball from those on the ground. The goalkeeper quickly resumes his starting position, and so on.

Variations

1. The coach gives the goalkeeper less time to react by shooting harder or standing closer to him.

2. Instead of starting in a standing position, the goalkeeper lies in the push-up position or face down or sits with his legs slightly apart before turning to face the coach.

• Reaction speed

Participants: 1 goalkeeper	Equipment: 6 balls
Coach	

147

Key aspects
- Reaction speed
- Agility
- Diving to stop low shots
- Diving to stop high to medium-high shots

- Rolling away to the side
- Take-off strength
- Catching the ball securely
- Deflecting the ball

Starting position
The goalkeeper stands with his legs slightly apart and with his back to the coach, who stands 4 yards behind him holding a ball. Another 5 balls lie on the ground 2 yards in front of the coach.

Phase 1
The goalkeeper throws the ball back hard through his legs, so that it reaches the coach at hip or knee height. The goalkeeper immediately turns to face the coach. (He turns alternately clockwise and counter-clockwise.)

Phase 2
The coach kicks the ball back to the goalkeeper, constantly varying the height, direction and speed of the ball. The goalkeeper catches the ball or deflects it. He takes the ball or picks up one of the balls from the ground and resumes his starting position, and so on.

Variations
The coach stands 12 yards behind the goalkeeper. The goalkeeper throws the ball 2-handed over his head so that it falls in front of the coach. The coach half-volleys it powerfully at the goalkeeper.

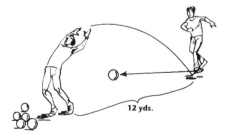

• **Reaction speed**

Participants:	1 goalkeeper Coach	Equipment:	6 balls

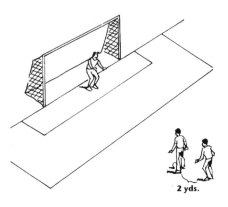

Starting position

The goalkeeper stands in the middle of the goal. The coach and the outfield player stand 20 yards outside the penalty area facing the goal. The outfield player stands 2 yards behind the coach, who has a ball at his feet.

2 yds.

Phase 1

The coach sprints toward the goal with the ball at his feet. The outfield player follows at a distance of 2 yards. Just before he reaches the 18-yard line the coach puts one foot on the ball to stop it and then sprints to one side leaving the ball behind him.

• Reaction speed

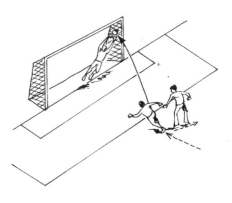

Phase 2

The outfield player immediately shoots on the run. The goalkeeper tries to stop the shot by catching, deflecting or punching it. If he catches it he throws it back to the coach, otherwise the outfield player runs and fetches it. Everyone resumes their starting positions, and so on.

Variations

1. The coach feints to stop the ball or backheel it and then shoots at goal himself on the run.
2. If the goalkeeper does not hold the shot, the coach follows up and tries to score from the loose ball.

• **Reaction speed**

Participants:	1 goalkeeper	Equipment:	1 ball
	1 outfield player		1 goal
	Coach		1 half of the pitch

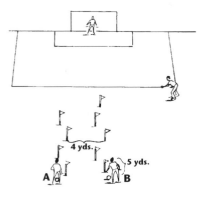

Starting position

The goalkeeper stands in the middle of the goal. Two outfield players stand 20 yards outside the penalty area facing the goal. Each has a ball at his feet. Between each of them and the 18-yard line is a zigzag line of marker flags. The right-hand line consists of 5 flags and the left-line consists of 4 flags. The 2 lines are 4 yards apart. The coach stands at the right-hand corner of the penalty area and calls out instructions when necessary.

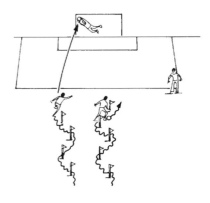

Phase 1

At a call from the coach, each player dribbles forward through his line of marker flags. Since player A only has to pass 4 flags he finishes first. As soon as he passes the last flag he shoots at goal. The goalkeeper tries to stop the ball by catching, deflecting or punching it. If he catches the ball he immediately rolls it away to the side.

• Reaction speed

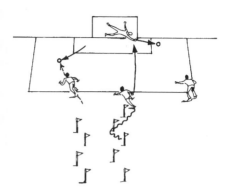

Phase 2
After dealing with the first shot the goalkeeper turns to player B, who shoots at goal after passing the fifth flag. He tries to place his shot so that the goalkeeper has a chance of reaching it. The goalkeeper tries to stop the shot. The outfield players run and fetch the balls back to the starting positions. The goalkeeper also resumes his starting position, and so on.

Variation
There are 5 flags in each line. The players therefore end their runs and shoot at goal almost simultaneously. To give the goalkeeper a chance of stopping both shots, they shoot at or close to his body.

• Reaction speed

Participants:	1 goalkeeper	Equipment:	2 balls
	2 outfield players		1 goal
	Coach		1 half of the pitch
			9 marker flags
		Variation:	10 marker flags

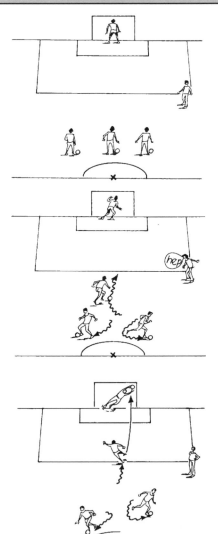

Starting position

The goalkeeper stands in the middle of the goal with his back to the pitch. Three outfield players stand 20 yards outside the penalty area facing the goal. Each has a ball at his feet. The coach stands at the right-hand corner of the penalty area and calls out instructions when necessary.

Phase 1

One of the outfield players runs at goal with the ball at his feet, while the other 2 outfield players dribble the ball around the pitch. The coach calls out when the first player arrives nears the penalty area.

Phase 2

When the coach calls out, the outfield player shoots at goal. At the same time the goalkeeper turns round and tries to stop the shot. He can catch, deflect or punch it. If he catches it he throws it back to the outfield player. The goalkeeper then resumes his starting position and the second outfield player starts his run at goal, and so on.

Variations

Instead of standing, the goalkeeper can be in the press-up position or he can lie face down on the ground or sit with his legs slightly apart.

• Reaction speed

Participants: 1 goalkeeper	**Equipment:** 3 balls
3 outfield players	1 goal
Coach	1 half of the pitch

Key aspects

- Reaction speed
- Agility
- Diving to stop low shots
- Diving to stop high to medium-high shots
- Rolling away to the side

- Take-off strength
- Catching the ball securely
- Punching the ball
- Deflecting the ball
- Defending with the feet

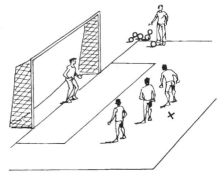

Starting position

The goalkeeper stands in the middle of the goal. The coach stands to his left at the point where the line marking the edge of the penalty area meets the goal line. He has a ball at his feet and another 5 balls are on the ground nearby. Three outfield players stand in a line 12 yards from the goal.

Phase 1

The coach crosses the ball low or medium-high to the outfield players, who must try to score with a first-time shot.

Phase 2

The goalkeeper stays on his line. He must try to anticipate the direction of the shot and block it with a reflex movement. The goalkeeper then resumes his starting position and the coach crosses the next ball, and so on.

Variations

1. The coach also hits high crosses, which the outfield players try to head into goal.
2. The outfield players also try to score if the ball runs loose after the first attempt.

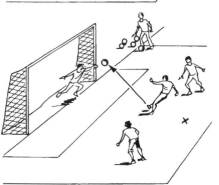

• Reaction speed

Participants:	1 goalkeeper	Equipment:	6 balls
	3 outfield players		1 goal
	Coach		1 penalty area

The authors

Gerd Thissen
Born 1951. Teacher of sport and French. Soccer teacher.
Scientific research and teaching assistant at the Institute for Sports Science of Aachen University of Technology since 1976. At the sociology department of Heinrich Heine University, Düsseldorf, since 1990. Member of the faculty of sports science of the Ruhr University, Bochum, since 1996.
Has coached youth, amateur and university soccer teams since 1968. Won the German University Championship 3 times with the Aachen University of Technology team. Teaches and lectures to coaches at regional and national soccer training courses and the annual courses of the Association of German Soccer Teachers.
Author of several books on the theory and practice of soccer with special emphasis on children's and youth soccer, goalkeeper coaching, teaching tactics and soccer-specific physical exercise.
Since 1997, West German Soccer Association's representative for cooperation between schools and clubs and member of the "General Coaching Plan for Child and Youth Soccer Players" Commission and the School Soccer Committee of the West German Soccer Association.
Publisher of sports books on soccer and ice hockey.

Klaus Röllgen
Born 1932. Graduate sports teacher.
Sports teacher with the Mittelrhein Soccer Association until 1998.
National winner of the German Soccer Association cup with the Mittelrhein Soccer Association team in 1974.
Author of several books on the coaching of technique and tactics in competitive soccer.
Employed by the German Soccer Association as a teacher of coaches. Lecturer at the national training courses of the Association of German Soccer Teachers and at coaches' congresses outside Germany.
President of the Association of German Soccer Teachers since 1994.

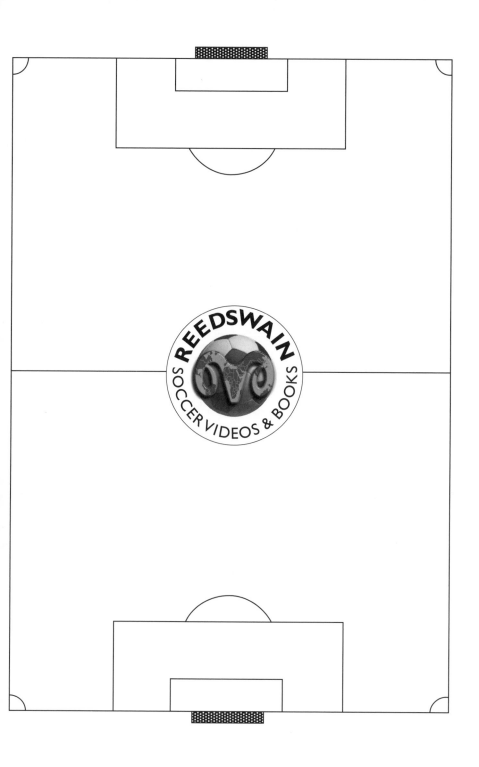

1-800-331-5191 • www.reedswain.com

NOTES

REEDSWAIN INC
612 Pughtown Road • Spring City PA 19475
1-800-331-5191 • www.reedswain.com

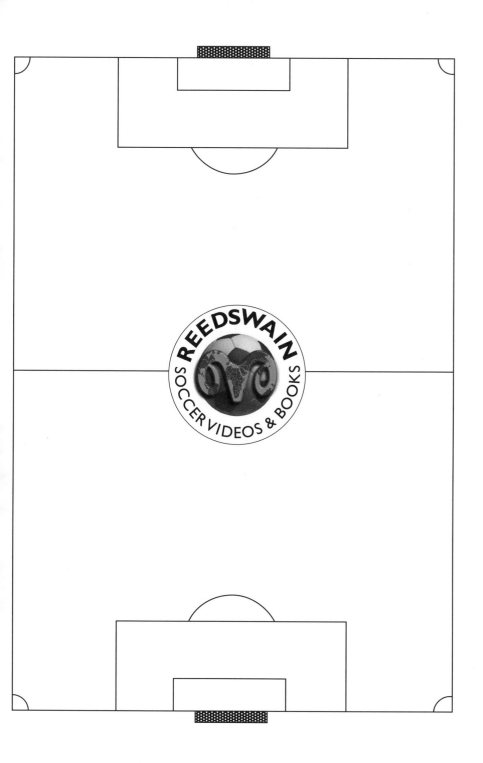

1-800-331-5191 • www.reedswain.com

REEDSWAIN BOOKS

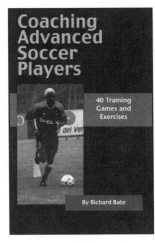

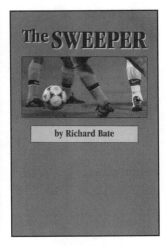

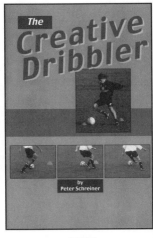

#169
Coaching Advanced Soccer Players
by Richard Bate
$12.95

#225
The Sweeper
by Richard Bate
$9.95

#256
The Creative Dribbler
by Peter Schreiner
$14.95

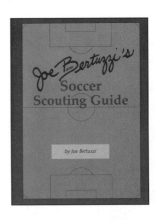

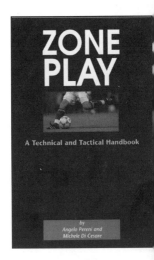

#789
The Soccer Scouting Guide
by Joe Bertuzzi
$12.95

#793
Coaching the 5-3-2 with a Sweeper
by Fascetti and Scaia
$14.95

#788
ZONE PLAY
A Technical and Tactical Handbook
$14.95